SEARCHINGS

SEARCHINGS

by

Gabriel Marcel

NEWMAN PRESS

NEW YORK   GLEN ROCK   WESTMINSTER

AMSTERDAM   TORONTO

This book was originally published in German by Verlag Knecht in 1964 under the title *Auf der Suche nach Wahrheit und Gerechtigkeit.* In this edition, Chapter V, "Martin Buber's Philosophical Anthropology," has been substituted for the original chapter, "I and the Other." All but one of the conferences that comprise this book were sponsored by the Catholic Student Community of Freiburg University, Germany, under the direction of Rev. Wolfgang Ruf, chaplain to the student community and editor of the German edition.

18091

Library of Congress
Catalog Card Number: 67-15716

Published by Newman Press
Editorial Office: 304 W. 58th St., N.Y., N.Y. 10019
Business Office: Westminster, Maryland 21157

Printed and bound in the
United States of America
by The Colonial Press, Clinton, Mass.

Contents

Foreword

Whether he speaks as a philosopher, dramatist or critic, Gabriel Marcel is motivated by a singularly intense concern for the existential predicament of the human person. That his philosophic writings are informal and unsystematic is only characteristic of his readiness to compromise a professionally meticulous "teaching" in favor of our initiation into an experiential participation in the very ground of being-in-the-world. This experience, in Marcel's own idiom, is "engagement"; it involves both freedom and obligation of the greatest magnitude. He is alert to seize every opportunity to make his experience available, to *exhibit himself,* in the noblest sense of the word. And he will not hesitate to use every available means to precipitate human dialogue. Of all the instruments in his repertory we have seriously neglected the unique importance of the lecture, as embodying the quintessence of self-display. From this aspect Marcel's lectures—and therefore the modest selection to follow—make a significant contribution to his collected works.

Marcel himself intimates as much by referring to them as "conferences." "Lecture" is quite inadequate to convey the essence of what actually happens. Faithful to the sense of the Latin word *confero,* Gabriel Marcel "collates" diverse thoughts from his many writings and unifies them in the form and structure of a conversation. His conferences are refreshingly direct; his thought and experience readily accessible.

The communication is a genuine sharing. He consigns his meaning to our hands, making us personally responsible for the transposition into our own intimate sphere of existence. Marcel is certainly not unware that man is on the brink, and he is bent on contributing toward "reintroducing the human element into a world precariously close to losing itself in hatred and a skein of abstractions."

Marcel's lecture tours are the expression of his thoroughly philosophical existence. He is a journeyer underway. The "other," the object of his *Searchings,* enjoys special priority, not the "I" that is a mere abstraction. Every conference finds him adapting to the ever-new present and the irreplaceable existences of his listeners here and now. In turn he expects a response, but never any two exactly alike.

Gabriel Marcel is a sensitive lover of music. I would not hesitate to compare him to David, who, by his "playing," exorcises evil spirits.

WOLFGANG RUF

I
In Search of
Truth and Justice

I will be the first to admit that this lecture is not going to be classical by any means. Since it has to do with a search I prefer to compare it to an adventurous voyage of discovery. This word "search," as I see it, ought to preface every other title of my philosophical writings, as it most aptly describes the way I think. This time I am searching for an adequate way to clarify the relationship between truth and justice. And this in face of the incontrovertible fact that apart from the efforts of a handful of philosophers the concepts "truth" and "justice" are generally tending to lose their significance. Naturally enough we want to counteract this tendency, but it means basing our efforts on experience that is particularly pertinent. With this in mind, the image of a voyage of discovery is perhaps less to the point than that of an assent.

I ask you not only to give me your attention but also to take an active part in a task that actually requires no vindication. In light of the unmistakable threats that keep cropping up, now aggressively, now in more insidious fashion, we Europeans are in duty bound not only to take stock of our fundamental merits, but also to embody these in an authentically militant consciousness. The order of the day is extreme watchfulness. If we neglect it in our thinking we are fated to perish in technocratic delirium, no matter what political form it assumes—as this is simply a matter of detail, not of essence.

Justice! Truth! I pronounce these words with particular reverence, but when I listen within I have to confess they evoke nothing more than a faint and muted echo. Or to use another image, these two words are like inscriptions carved into the facade of a public building; we simply pass them by, no more moved at the sight of them than we are by anything else that has degenerated into commonplace.

Yet, I am sure that under certain circumstances deep within me this monotonous and deceptive apparition could give way to inexorable reality. More precisely, in a definite situation I could be aroused from my apathy to perform deeds of profound consequence, simply because "truth" and "justice" of a sudden become suffused with irresistible appeal. Of course, I can only speak for myself. It is my personal conviction. Yet, I have to ask myself whether at my age I am still actually capable of experiencing such violent emotion and assuming such responsibilities. At the same time I do know from experience that if I were to evade the issue at the last moment, I would have to judge my behavior most severely. I would have to regard it as a blatant disavowal of everything I have always stood for.

Let me repeat; I am only speaking for myself. I know there are other people—although I do not know who they are or their numbers—who as things now stand would remain deaf to a similar appeal. Without the slightest feeling of remorse they would say that such big words as these no longer make much sense in our day and age. Yes, some will even protest that courage means being aware of this very fact and not letting oneself be carried away to reckless deeds for the sake of notions that have permanently forfeited their significance.

These remarks suffice to place us on a plane of thought that has nothing to do with discursive thinking. It is not my present purpose to cull from the works of philosophers, past or present, their considerations about justice or truth and then in a work similar to theirs manipulate my findings so as to present some sort of resounding consensus. I hardly think this would manage to arouse anyone. I rather think it is a question of waking up, or more precisely of arousing *ourselves*. For if what I said above is true, it indicates that we in the West are in a general state of deep spiritual torpor as far as truth and justice are concerned. And perhaps all the more so because we live in a well-ordered and regulated—I might almost say, a neatly pigeonholed—environment where life is lived on a broader plane and under almost perfectionized stipulations.

Here I am going to speak from my own experience, for I would like this conference to rest on personal testimony. During the years immediately prior to the First World War, I first began to think for myself and to create a personal approach to the intellectual lands that I was later to discover. At the time, I hardly thought problems of justice could arouse any heated controversy. All sensible people, or those who had reached a certain degree of intellectual maturity, were unanimous in their desire to find a reasonable solution to these problems. And "reasonable," I thought, meant of course "extremely boring."

It seems strange that I could have thought like that in my youth; for my childhood was influenced by the Dreyfus affair and it even brought discord into our close family circle. Although I was only a small boy at the time, I passionately sided with the Dreyfus supporters and attacked with just as much animation those who were annoyed at seeing the country thrown into disorder and the army discredited just because one individual had merely been sent to prison—innocent of the crime, perhaps, but still a very antipathetic creature.

Order was eventually restored, a monotonous order at that, without glamor and, I might almost say, without interest. About 1908 or 1910 I thought only brainless people could still deny that the manner of procedure against the unfortunate Dreyfus was contemptible. After the miscarriage of the review trial, he was pardoned by the president of the Republic; but this supposedly palliative action satisfied nobody. And the lackluster expediency had repercussions in the quarter of Paris where I grew up. It was predominantly bourgeois and hardly what you would call picturesque; but its law enforcement left nothing to be desired. When I try to recall what motivated my thinking in

those days, it seems to have been an irrepressible protest against
that depersonalized order—and let me repeat, it was an extremely
bland order at that.

But I lacked the temperament of an anarchist; besides, I suffered from an innate horror of crowds and popular uprisings.
My antipathy was only increased and intensified, perhaps, by
my premature reading about the French Revolution. This is
surely a very clear indication that Socialism did not appeal to
me. Therefore, all my protesting had to be done within the area
of metaphysical and religious thinking, and that precisely because my parents, both agnostics, had reared me without any
Church affiliation. When I look back at my boyhood attitude it
naturally appears quite romantic, for it was more or less in opposition to the new "enlightenment" I vowed to withstand. Still,
I would have been very astonished if someone at that time had
told me I was the romantic type; for in those days the word was
charged with overtones and associations that in no way harmo-
nized with what I thought about myself. If someone had
approached me on this, I would have replied: Today we are
called to overcome the outdated antithesis between Classicism
and Romanticism; to perpetuate it is scarcely in keeping with
our present level of culture. To an extent I would have been
right; but in view of our present context I have to admit anything that had to do with justice I then thought depended on
the intellect and had to be judged by it, so to speak. Certainly
the events of 1914 altered my view of things profoundly. I have
to confess I understood nothing about what was actually brew-
ing at the time. I was deceived by the apparent stability of our
state of social and political affairs, so much so I naively imagined
it could be prolonged indefinitely. Then all of a sudden emotive
questions began stirring in my mind: Was justice and genuine
right on our side? I was convinced they were, and yet I had to
admit our opponents were equally convinced of the just nature of
their own cause. Were they honestly convinced, or were they
simply misled by passion? At this point I would like to say that
the chauvinism of the period fostered an active antipathy in
me. I considered it eminently important to distinguish it
from authentic, enlightened patriotism. I well remember that I

was deeply vexed when I saw such a great personage as Bergson writing bitter accusations against Germanism and uttering passionate judgments against great artists like Wagner, whom I admired.

Later on, I was confronted by other problems that had to do with justice. One of my fellow students, a young philosopher whose outstanding gifts of mind and character I greatly admired, got into trouble when he sent pacifist pamphlets to the front in 1917. To some extent the pamphlets probably did help incite the bloody riot that followed the collapse of the offensive on April 16, 1916, and, indirectly, the subsequent brutal repression. Shortly thereafter, I wrote the first act of a play that was never completed entitled *A Just Man*. It dealt with the problem of "conscientious objectors," as they later came to be called. As might be expected I offered a solution based on national conformism. It seemed intolerable that a man should use pamphlets to induce soldiers at the front to desert and thus make themselves liable to the death penalty, without assuming any personal risk himself. But I also knew that my friend would have been ready to assume any and every risk, even the death penalty, if it had come to that. So while I condemned him in my play, he still enjoyed my personal esteem. Even though I was not yet a Christian—and had no intention of becoming one—I did question the ideals of peace and brotherhood in the name of which my friend had called for rebellion. I also suspected that a rebellion might conceivably have fostered the imperialistic designs of the enemy. For that reason I thought it should be soundly condemned as absurd and profoundly contradictory. Twenty years later in the face of Hitler's growing might, I had to pronounce a similar verdict against the pacifism that was becoming noticeable in a growing number of French circles. I recall that I did not agree with Emanuel Mounier on this very point when Friedrich Wilhelm Foerster exposed the pitfall that eventually awaited the pacifists.

Whatever happened, questions of justice remained alive in me ever since 1914. Therefore, I was deeply perturbed when some time ago in an otherwise flattering article in *L'Express,* the writer expressed regret that I have bothered so little about questions of justice and perhaps thereby have made myself guilty of what he called "a betrayal from above." My immediate reaction was that I should set things straight. But I then realized that my concern for justice, which doubtless has grown stronger over the years and which certainly must have resulted from my childhood stand in the Dreyfus affair, evidently did not stand out clearly enough from the mass of ideas I had expressed in my various published writings. I am referring only to my philosophical writings; in my plays, in *L'Emissaire*, for example, the problem of justice is put clearly enough.

Please excuse me for tarrying so long on my reminiscences. But I think it was necessary; and, in fact, it prepared the way for a very important observation. It is extraordinarily dangerous to consider justice as existing outside of a "existential relationship," or, to speak less technically, a relationship outside of drama. For in drama one deals with passion, and one crystallizes a situation that arouses a unique passion—namely, "the passion for justice and truth."

But now to the essence of our present inquiry! I want to clarify the relationship between justice and truth. And yet I am not at all sure that I can accomplish the task under conditions you and I will find similarly acceptable. But with the world the way it is today, it just has to be done, precisely because in many civilized countries we can clearly discern an insidious devaluation of important concepts, where even such fundamental notions like truth and justice are at times maliciously called into question.

Now we must investigate *truth*. Very many people nowadays, even faithful Christians, or at least those who consider themselves faithful, could with ease adopt the question of Pontius Pilate: What is truth? The splendid development of technical science in the last fifty years has fostered what I call "depreciatory questioning." A famous scientist, Prince Louis de Broglie, said to me a few years ago: "The difference between science and technology is gradually disappearing. That means that nowadays the rules of science are being sought less in a truth one is striving to establish, than in the experimental potentialities latent in the formulas the scientist discovers in the meantime.

This does not mean that pragmatism, as it was defined at the beginning of the century, particularly in the United States, has already triumphed. I hardly think we need go that far. The problem of truth simply seems to be losing its importance. Men might still be willing to recognize partial truths, but they find it extremely difficult to establish any kind of systematic relationship between them. Rather contemptuously, they leave it to the philosopher to perform the perilous task, and they show little interest in it themselves. What actually prevails is not pragmatism, but a pluralism of facts, which are only on rare occasions formulated as a doctrine. But even then, we have a contradiction on our hands. It would be a case of stratified thinking; and stratified thinking, as we know, ultimately requires that the stratified elements be subsumed into a unity. Slowly but surely we are becoming aware of the general "indolence" that pervades our quest for truth, just as it did our search for justice. This point deserves our careful attention. I know of only two instances where such indolence gives way to the opposite disposition of fanaticism. I have in mind Marxist dogmatism (where it crystallizes into a form of Neo-Koranism) and theological dogmatism (where it crystallizes into the attitude: Outside Thomism there is no salvation).

At this point philosophical reflection has to take advantage of its rights and protest sharply against this kind of thinking, for it plainly amounts to an act of violence. While it might be true that such dogmatizing is based on thoroughly understandable dialectical principles, it nonetheless risks evoking in those who simply cannot accept it just the opposite disposition. I would call it "debility," but it could just as well be called "infraskepticism," since it amounts to a skepticism that is even incapable of proceeding skeptically. Instead, consciousness withdraws into a fog that stifles courageous initiative, and a sense of responsibility is replaced by fundamental mistrust. Needless to say, this is the kind of attitude that encourages the numerous systems of oppression everywhere in evidence today.

Perhaps now we can see that dogmatic Marxism and an overly dogmatic philosophy are existentially similar at root—and we have already seen briefly to what they can lead, namely, spiritual indolence. And I frankly think this same debility has also affected our respect for justice and truth.

Now, I am sure this will provoke some lively protest. After all are we not making many more demands today in the name of justice? Is this evidence of indolence? Why, we even have unions and other organized groups, in fact whole nations, protesting that justice be done. I will admit this is a very difficult question and it has to be treated with delicacy. For example, a group of workers demands higher wages, giving as its reason the higher cost of living. Offhand we would agree that the workers' demands are justified. Still, those who are responsible for the general economic situation can say that, while the demands are indeed justified, granting them would only lead to renewed demands that would eventually damage the general economy of the country and inflict injury on the general citizenry. In a case like this it seems very difficult to know whether a distinctly *just demand* and an *apparent justice* might not eventually lead to real injustice.

If we went into this question at length, we would see it involves problems of social technique of such intricacy that in their objective form they can hardly be voiced by any one particular group of workers. Consequently, isolated demands are not necessarily prompted by love or concern for genuine justice; they rather arise from a host of assorted interests and from needs that are more or less acute. But because everyone judges his own isolated case, there is, in effect, no judgment at all. For a judgment worthy of the name consists in disregarding oneself. One might even say that the responsible authorities, namely government officials, are the only ones who can take justice into account. But that does not mean that the equity they establish, or are supposed to establish, necessarily deserves the name justice, either.

For the moment let us put aside the problem as it has to do with the government and the common welfare, and look at the question as the individual sees it. Here, I feel, a concern for justice is only genuine if it leads to a protest that is not inspired by partisan interest. In fact, partisan concern might well even hurt rather than help those who voice it.

People are going to have to experience not only a development, but what actually amounts to a puzzling confusion between justice and equity. The two notions have to be kept separate, especially nowadays, when the notion of a just distribution of goods is becoming so important. It seems we are just a step away from speaking of an *equal* distribution of goods. Every mother knows how violently even a small child reacts when she divides a cake and appears to favor someone else at the table. Rather than precipitate a quarrel she will take great pains to cut the cake into equal pieces. She will even divide the fruit on the cake evenly, if there be any, or find some way of compensating for any possible inequality in the distribution. However, it is very doubtful that concessions of this sort possess any authentic ethical value. While she might justify her behavior on practical grounds, sober consideration will hardly reveal any further reasonable grounds for her precaution. In fact, not to leave our example, it is not even certain that there is reason for treating everyone at the table alike. The only thing we can say is that if I do not bother about equal distribution, there will be no end of quarreling; therefore, it is better to play safe.

I am sure one could just as easily apply the same considerations to the question of universal suffrage, for instance, even though it has nothing to do with just distribution as such. Does it make sense to say that an illiterate or an alcoholic has the same right to vote as a professor, a doctor, or a public official? Certainly not! The term "justice" is used here in a diluted sense, and it would not stand up under careful scrutiny. From a rational point of view, the most one could say is that on purely practical grounds, that need not all be convincing, the concept "equality" would make better sense in this context.

But is there any question of values? The solution is more one of "do-or-die," arising from the fact that any kind of legal discrimination would occasion endless quarreling or might eventually lead to civil war. Still, it is unmistakable: doing justice on the basis of equity is no more than a fiction; it is a subterfuge pure and simple. Our example is somewhat unfortunate because universal suffrage has so completely won out in so-called democratic countries that no one would even think of questioning the principle upon which this subterfuge rests. A second example is more to the point, namely, that of the United Nations. Can we for one moment accept the assertion that it is *just* to grant the same right of dissent to States whose people are 80 to 90 per cent illiterate as to highly cultured States? Any unprejudiced person will see at once that this kind of equivalence is unreal. It appears even more unreal if we take into account that we cannot even begin to compare States with living people. For many States are nothing more than social agglomerations with no stable character which are subject to rapid dissolution.

The fact, therefore, strikes us forcibly: Whenever we find ourselves involved in an unreal situation, we cannot expect to be able to speak of justice realistically. Furthermore, I think I see a negative relationship between truth and justice; and that is what today's lecture proposes to explain. We also understand why our functionalized world, in which everyone is hardly anything more than a digit, is becoming more and more impervious to a direct feeling of justice. I might almost say that justice has already degenerated to the point where it consists of little more than a price-list of sorts, a chart, especially where it has anything to do with punishments. We even have specialists who assess charges and then recommend that their findings be applied to one or the other particular case. But it would seem that the charts hardly correspond to anything resembling a genuine feeling of guilt. Courts of justice nowadays inspire people with no more respect than do revenue offices. The judge is no longer recognized as a man of justice. And I feel that when respect is destroyed, justice itself is bound to vanish.

Now, somebody might feel prompted to accuse me of nihilism or at least of agnosticism in this area. But at this point a distinction is in order: One may well believe that today's system of justice, with its attendant enforcement machinery, actually has nothing to do with justice in the real sense of the word. This does not mean, however, that this machinery could not be progressively improved; on the contrary, it can and must be im-

proved. Still, it would be naive to believe that this would ultimately lead to justice, for the simple yet profound reason that
the judgment of one man concerning another is always bound to
contain a measure of injustice. With that said, I will certainly be
asked to define what I mean by a justice that can in any way coin-
cide with the apparatus for administering justice. For example,
I can be called to explain the reasons for my criticism of equality
and of egalitarianism. Can we, for example, assert that true justice means treating everyone according to his deserts and his
abilities? But, then, how can merits and capabilities be justly ap-
praised? Upon reflection we see that any appraisal we might
make can only be approximate, and, at that, it can be very deceptive.

Furthermore, it is not permissible to judge living persons at
one particular point in their lives, as though they could never
rise beyond this point. A pertinent example would be to treat
the so-called undeveloped nations as if they were absolutely
incompetent to participate actively in determining the present
and future fate of mankind. That would be to isolate them in
their present condition instead of helping them to work their
way out of it. On the other hand (and this brings us back to earlier remarks), are we really assisting them to rise above their present restrictions by encouraging them to make unwarranted
demands and treating them as if they had and should have the
same rights as the so-called civilized nations? It all comes down
to this: true justice depends on the *spirit* in which we undertake
whatever educational activity is designed to promote their development. We might actually give authentic justice the lie by
trying to define it through an evaluation of the concrete data—
no matter how correct our evaluation might be. The popular
image of scales in this connection is very instructive. And while
we might often think it quite apt, we know very well that it is
hardly the true picture of justice at all. We are reminded of the
well-known saying: *summum jus, summa injuria.* George
Simmel once said that life is more than simply living. And I
think we can apply this analogously to the concept of justice.
To express the idea even more clearly, we can say that justice
is not justice unless, from a certain point onward, it is also the

beginning of sympathy, or, in its deepest reality, the beginning of love.

And yet our conscience tells us: If justice must necessarily include love, it may by no means be confused with it. Why so? Because justice requires that we do many things for which we have no affective attraction. Let me cite an extreme example from actual experience. A French Communistic university professor was accused of conniving with the Algerian Freedom Front; he was imprisoned and then disappeared under circumstances that gave rise to sinister rumors. I was among those who claimed that those who pronounced sentence on the conduct of the professor were still obligated to give a full explanation for his disappearance. Further, I maintained that those who were responsible for his disappearance, that is, for his death, should be subjected to punitive measures, and these punishments should be made known to the public. It is not sufficient that protest and accusation against this state of affairs should come only from those who approve of the behavior of the professor, that is, from Communists. Furthermore, a strict distinction has to be made between the condemnation of what might be considered treasonable conduct and the means by which the enraged representatives of the law forced this supposed traitor to speak, and finally killed him.

In an example like this, several main features of justice stand out clearly; first, interior independence from any subjective inclinations. More important is a respect for a person's inviolability. Precisely this second feature is to be emphasized, for nowadays it seems to be the aspect most frequently misunderstood. Inviolability ultimately means the sanctified character that is insolubly bound up with the fact that the prisoner is an unarmed man in the hands of his enemies. Precisely because this man is unarmed, the human, almost irresistible temptation is to destroy him by force and, particularly, to extract admissions from him. To emphasize his inviolability is to erect an absolute barrier between this temptation and the execution of what it insinuates. Nothing better proves that justice can never be reduced to a social technique of any kind whatsoever. This statement of inviolability is essentially meta-technical; it exists to

establish an absolute boundary for the techniques used in dealing with the prisoner. And expediency is no excuse. How often
do we hear that the necessities of war compel the forces of law
and order to carry out some particular measure that cannot be
defended legally. But the simple fact of the matter is that such
practices simply cannot be reconciled with authentic justice; they
only place the one who implements them on the same plane
with the one whom he condemns.

The significance of these remarks within our present context
consists in pointing up the close relationship between justice and
the holy. Only now do we see that this *holy consciousness* of justice has pervaded the criticism I have made so far. On this plane,
and only on this plane, the relationship between justice and
truth begins to shine through.

We now have to clarify the notion of truth in a similar manner. Rather than calling this a definition of terms, I would prefer to speak of a liberation of the notion of truth. We have to
emancipate ourselves from the routine which daily life threatens
to foist upon us, where the ideas of justice, the sacred, and truth
stand in danger of being bereft of all meaning. Though it is difficult to avoid, the word "idea" hardly strikes me as being very
appropriate, since justice, truth and the sacred are not to be
put on the purely ideational level. The sacred must be considered as the root and the fundamental term of reference for
both justice and truth. To the extent that life is desecrated, the
values of justice and truth dry up and are completely without
lifeblood.

No matter how one defines the sacred, no matter what forms
it could assume (or still does assume in societies we rightly or
wrongly designate as primitive), it is still clear in our mind that,
independent of all adherence to a particular religion, there can
be nothing sacred that is not subject to a supreme and absolute
tribunal. To go a step further, this tribunal may not be limited
to something that Fichte, for example, designates as "moral
world order." Otherwise, the word "sacred" cannot really have
its full meaning; an order may certainly be worthy of *recogni-*

tion, but recognition can never be mistaken for the *sacred.* I am inclined to believe that it is only when we can actually perceive a word, or something that corresponds to a word, in the comprehensive sense of λόγος, that the word "sacred" assumes its full meaning. Is not this word, this sovereign word, and the transcendent "ego" that it generates, the sole source of all that we call justice and truth?

Perhaps this will be clearer to us if we carefully consider the notion of an oath. I think it is here that I perceive the oneness of these three basic data that are so often separated by the analytical mind. What, then, does it mean for a man to live in truth and according to truth? In answer let me first consider what it does not mean; unquestionably, man can certainly live in peace with an order that is imposed upon him from without, a totalitarian State, for example. But if he maintains that this unfortunate state of affairs is a *true* mode of being, he is grossly overlooking the fact that only something that is spiritual deserves the name "truth."—But that still is not clear enough. Let us perhaps proceed now from a negative point of view. To live according to truth means not to live according to one's moods. How so? Moods are variable, even for the individual who lives his whole life according to them. But when we use the word "truth," no matter how we define it, it always refers to something that shows consistency and absolute stability. In any case, living according to truth means bringing oneself into agreement—but not only with oneself (as this would perhaps mean only a formal coherence). No, it means bringing ourselves into agreement with a demand which has to express itself in us and cannot be stifled. While experience shows that we can stifle it if we want to, it nonetheless resides in the very nature of this demand that it should be clarified. This does not necessarily mean that the demand must press forward into consciousness in entire universal character. Most probably it will only take shape when a particular situation demands it, or when an action is required, regardless of the personal risk involved.

Let me give another example: A member of the French Council of State was in direct contact with Marshal Petain for a long time during the period of German occupation. During Petain's trial he felt personally obliged to speak in the marshal's behalf, whatever it might cost him personally. As was to be feared, because of the atmosphere within the French administrative bodies at the time, he was, if my memory serves me correctly, suspended for two years because he had testified in favor of a man whose fate had already been determined. Consequently, both he and his large family were forced to live under most difficult material conditions for the duration.

We might say he was only following his conscience. But despite the superficial note this unfortunate phrase evokes, the case in point had to do with genuine truth, and consequently it was something spiritual. If this man had refrained from testifying out of prudence or fear, he would have acted contrary to this spiritual character of truth and, at the same time, would have committed an injustice. In this example, we see how justice and truth come very close to each other. But this man was, after all, a faithful Christian, and, doubtless, he was living on the plane of the holy; otherwise, his obligation would not have impelled him to act as he did. It is most likely that he prayed for light before making his decision, and, under the impulse of what he understood as an answer to his prayer, he resolved to intervene in a manner that was contrary to his own and his family's interests.

I have often pondered this example; and I am sure it will help you recognize more clearly the relationship I see between justice and truth. In another context I called this relationship the "creative testimony" that amounts to the fundamental vocation of man. If our being-in-the-world has a meaning, it can be that history itself is that very process in which we are personally called upon to give our testimony. Perhaps I have not sufficiently emphasized this in my writings, but in *The Mystery of Being* I do say:

Doubtless, the testimony that we have to give extends to the concrete historical situation. Neither a mathematician nor a physicist can be a witness. This is because, in a certain regard, they appear as the arena where a particular truth reveals itself. This truth is so constituted that it relegates the world, or the bearer of truth, which it needs at a definite point of time, to the realm of what is purely contingent. On the other hand, where the witness intervenes and becomes necessary as witness, it is only he who bears this testimony and endows it with importance. He is, however, a living being who comes to life at a very definite moment of history.

But today I am tempted to ask whether the opposition between the truth of the mathematician and that of the witness ought not be resolved. The scientist, insofar as he is genuinely creative, can also be a witness, for he attests to the worth of his discovery in the face of those who would dispute, or at least undervalue, its significance.

But one cannot speak about testimony without mentioning the transcendent reality that actually utters the testimony. This transcendence is truth, insofar as it resists every effort to objectify it. Naturally, the irresistible temptation of all positivistic spirits is to confuse transcendence with humanity in its totality. But I believe it is easy to show the untenability of this notion. It understands totality only in its extensive sense; as soon as we take the spiritual character of man into account, it is simply impossible to add men like so many stones or blocks of wood. We have to forego any notion of addition and eventually have to hold to what one might call "man" or "humanity." Besides, we should be aware of how even the idea of "man" is possible, and whether it does not, for example, presuppose a divine understanding within which framework it has its appointed place. This is no time to take a stand on the question, so I will simply observe that it is becoming more and more obvious that we can only speak of transcendence within this particular context.

Someone could justifiably ask what makes up the creative testimony of someone who has left behind no great accomplishments. Again an example might indicate where the answer lies.

I do not know if you have learned from experience, as I have, that certain incidents drop into our lives like inspirations, and, like these, they are sudden and unforeseeable. At the same time they fall like a seal beneath a long process of indefinite, interior preparation. Just as I was writing these lines, in fact, something came to mind that ought to clarify what I have rather timidly tried to express.

No doubt, some of you have heard about the miners in the Ruhr valley of Germany who became resolute champions of Moral Rearmament; they wrote a play to articulate their experience and were very outspoken whenever referring to their conversion. It premiered in Berlin before hundreds of people in the Russian occupied zone, and then it was played in England and France. After a lengthy conference with Chancellor Adenauer in Bonn, during which he recommended they continue to remind the French of the wounds inflicted on their country by National Socialism, they decided to perform an act of reparation in Paris.

When I learned of their intention I advised them to select for this affair Mount Valérian, the fortress that dominates Paris, the place of execution for more than 4,500 resistance fighters. We were able to secure three of the most prominent resistance fighters, who had been taken to Germany, and received them at what had in meantime become a veritable shrine for all Frenchmen. I had the good fortune to participate in this simple, touching ceremony. On the esplanade, where the large monument to the resistance fighters now stands, the author of the play declared in the name of his comrades that here in the presence of the invisible victims they acknowledged the entire guilt that rests on the German people, and that they were obligating themselves to do everything possible to prevent the repetition of such a horrible crime. If I now recall the December morning on which these decisive words were uttered, it is because, at this precise moment, in a flash of intuition, I recognized the relation between truth and justice that I have just attempted to explain to you by such torturous paths of reflection.

The event was primarily an act of authentic justice. It had come alive before our very eyes on this December morning when this group of innocent people assumed a genuine obligation. Their unostentatious pledge was intended to restore an order for which men and women had courageously stood up and freely sacrificed their lives. We may also say that these men and women, some of them Communists, others Christians, still others unclassified, sacrificed their lives for a just cause. But where does truth come in? We have to ask this question for the resistance fighters who became martyrs, as well as for the witnesses who came as pilgrims to offer an act of atonement. But a difficulty arises. I told you that the resistance fighters were far from unanimous in their religious convictions. So where is truth? Behind this question lies the erroneous idea that truth has to be identified with a specific doctrine or "ism." If this were true some of the resistance fighters would have fought in the name of truth, others in the name of error. The unity we thought we recognized here dissolves; or are we about to fall into a theory of destructive relativism?

Now, we have to distinguish carefully between truth and the various and sundry ways of viewing life. What was common to all was more than a rejection—that would be much too little; it was the fact that they fully, completely and resolutely stood behind this rejection. Thus, the rejection became a fact; it became embodied in existence and developed a whole series of consequences of such importance that each individual's rejection became his fate.

Let no one object that we are now in the realm of existence and not in that of truth. For this is precisely the contradiction that has to be abolished. One cannot deny that all these people, differing so much from one another, were yet, as a group, illumined by the same light and united by a common brotherly bond. What was this light but the idea that humanity had to be restored to its dignity? The light in this case is invisible because it is the very source of light; it makes seeing possible. And what do we understand here by "seeing" but, primarily, the proper evaluation of the options available to us? Divergent views are possible only when objectifying thinking takes over, as in the case of Marxism and various brands of inferior theology.

This is the light that illuminated the Germans on that December morning. And the mystery of this encounter—and it was truly an encounter—lies in the fact that these people swore an oath and bound themselves in a timeless agreement with those who had given their lives on this very same spot.

We must pursue this line of thought further. On the night before their execution, many of the condemned scratched some words on the walls of the abandoned chapel where they were imprisoned. Many expressed a vehement desire for the inevitable revenge to come. But revenge as such is always unjust. It becomes justice only when it purifies itself, and when it rises resplendent in the garb of repentance and free resolve. On that morning a spiritual climate became a reality in which the deepest pain and the purest joy embraced in mystic union.

You would not be satisfied if I ended my lecture with this image, striking as it is. Doubtless you feel I should draw some practical conclusions from it, and so I will.

What seems to stand out most clearly in these considerations and examples is that one can hardly speak of justice and truth without making reference to a vocation of some kind.

Certainly the call can be misunderstood; man can certainly remain deaf to every appeal if he wants to. This only goes to show that liberty is very closely woven into everything we have said on this particular subject. To fail against justice implies contributing to, or fostering in oneself and others, everything that opposes this appeal, this vocation. But it also means being responsible for concealing or excluding truth, insofar as truth is spirit and light.

In the last analysis, these relationships cannot be either seen or interpreted without the clear light of revelation. And yet they can also be perceived by men of goodwill for whom revelation is still a dead letter.

Someone may ask whether I have not introduced the idea of the sacred in order to have it serve as a bridge between justice and truth. Yes, I did. But the "sacred" supersedes every assent to a specific credo, even if one is certainly able to interpret it in the light of higher certitudes. Let us recall what I said by way of introduction: We are living in a world where, under the pressure of technology and its practitioners, reverence for the oath is waning. This is merely a further indication of the general profanization of the world. I have known people who have preserved in themselves this regard for the sacred in all its strictness, and yet, metaphysically, referred to themselves as unbelievers. One might say that these people were believers without realizing it. That may be true; but if we consider them existentially and in the perspective of their personal approach to knowledge, we shall have to admit that we have no right to stress the personal, implicit belief that they reject.

In general, we can only say that those intermediate steps to which men and women of lofty moral character in the last century and the beginning of this could still hold appear to be violently shaken. An abyss seems to yawn between men who have lost every notion of the fundamental connection I have endeavored to point out to you because of materialism, and believers who profess their faith and for whom these truths can in no way be separated from the single reality that is the living God.

Honest as well as hypocritical attempts have been made to bridge the chasm. Some people are even whispering that Marxism and Christianity—a very special kind of Christianity—are not irreconcilable opposites. One can only say, as I did to a Communist several weeks ago at the microphone, that as long as we are disputing abstractions and "isms," we may say what we please. But such declarations possess no value and no meaning. The problem becomes real, and people begin to know what we are talking about, only when we refer to concrete situations. And what about the people who exist behind the Iron Curtain? How can one overlook the fact that here there is a genuine question of truth and justice? I have been assured regarding both Poland and Hungary, that the uprisings were directed particularly against the lies which were constantly and shamelessly broadcast by an enslaved radio. But this very enslavement provides evidence of a basic injustice that cannot even recognize itself as such.

You need not offer the objection that there are also plenty of lies and injustices on our side of the Iron Curtain. I am not about to deny that. But one can still expose these lies and injustices in the West, and hope that, in the long run, we will eventually enjoy partial relief. But in the East European countries, where the lie has become law, all such hope is vain. And yet these unmitigated systems of oppression still dare to call themselves democracies.

This concluding observation of my lecture should spur you

on to pursue this thought further. You will pardon me for having put your attention and your patience to such a difficult test. But in light of this remark we will see the essentially ambiguous twilight that nowadays characterizes the West. To the extent we indulge in self-satisfaction, and smugly boast of our accomplishments, we become guilty of blindness and even of the lie. And we can expect the enemy to profit from our misbehavior. The contrary will be true only if the West wakes up to its internal imperfections and rudely unmasks the practical materialism that threatens its existence. Only on condition that it resolutely measures up to its vocation—a vocation that lies at the root of all its real accomplishments—may it harbor the hope of surviving a struggle whose stake is salvation or downfall.

II
Science and Wisdom

In order to make clear what it is I propose to speak about to-day under the broad title "Science and Wisdom," I will first have to elaborate upon some of the notions involved.

What significance are we to assign to wisdom in an age so patently controlled by science, or by the innumerable techniques that go to make it up? What novel attitude toward life is the hegemony of science and technology likely to create? Is wisdom liable to degenerate into a list of technical processes and thereby relinquish the outstanding value that moralists of the past have assigned to it?

Now, if I did not choose for my lecture a more precise title like "Science and Wisdom in the Modern World," it is simply because I hardly assumed we could discuss our theme without making at least some reference to the history of thought. Obviously, any elaborate reconstruction of the history of the problem is out of the question in a lecture as short as this. To do it justice we would have to investigate what the Epicureans and the Stoics, and Plato, had to say on the matter. But since, as I say, this is impossible for the moment, I am going to limit myself to mentioning relevant points from the thought of the seventeenth century—and from Descartes in particular—analyzing them and then, in a summary fashion, describing how the problem developed in the eighteenth century and later as a result of Romanticism and the success of revolutionary ideas.

In the foreword to the French edition of the *Principles of Philosophy* we find weighty texts that excellently characterize some important aspects of Descartes' wide range of ideas. I quote: "The word philosophy means a study of wisdom, and by wisdom one ought to understand not only cleverness in undertakings but a complete knowledge of all things that man can know, for the conduct of his own life, for the preservation of his health and for the invention of the arts." He adds that this knowledge is to be deduced from fundamental sources, and proceeds to show how "the wisdom that men usually possess is actually acquired." (This is evident enough: Descartes' wisdom is the result of experience through the senses, conversation with other men, books written by people who are in a position to teach us worthwhile lessons.) In this same foreword we read as well the famous sentence: "All philosophy is a tree; its roots are metaphysics, its trunk is physics and the branches stemming from this trunk are all the other sciences. These can be reduced to the three major sciences, namely, medicine, mechanics, and morality: I mean the highest and most perfect morality, which presupposes a complete mastery of the other types of knowledge and is the highest degree of wisdom."

It is remarkable just how broad an interpretation Descartes assigns the notion of wisdom. One might almost say wisdom is coextensive with knowing. He seems to presume that if man makes progress in knowledge, he will at the same time soar into the realm of morality. But I for one would have some reservations on the matter. Descartes is far from identifying intellect and will. The will in itself is unlimited; it is not intellectual capacity; and this is the distinction that makes error, especially moral error, possible.

My colleague and friend Henri Gouhier, one of the most accomplished Descartes scholars, called my attention to a letter addressed to Father Mesland (and not to Mersenne, as stated in the Pléiade edition) that is dated February 9, 1645. Here, Descartes speaks of the freedom of indifference. He writes:

I have been far from ever denying that the will possesses this positive characteristic [namely, freedom of indifference];

in my opinion we come face to face with it not only whenever the will decides upon an activity to which it is not driven by force of a reason favoring one side over the other, but also in every other act of the will; the will never decides without bringing it into play. Thus we are free to do something even though it is dictated by a very evident reason and (from a moral standpoint) we could hardly do the opposite. Absolutely speaking, you see, we are free to pursue a good that we clearly recognize as such, or free to recognize an evident truth if in our opinion it is a good that will manifest the freedom of our independent choice.

Spinoza's thought represents a species of radical intellectualism: will and intellect are one and the same thing. The idea of the wise man is one of absolute simplicity and coherence. The wise man is the one who has freed himself from the snares of imagination and the yoke of passion. However, it is the work of the intellect that frees him. "In the degree that the spirit understands all things as necessary, its power over the passions is increased and it frees itself from their yoke" (Sentence 6 of Book 5 of *Ethics*). Of course, it should be evident that Spinoza is not speaking as a psychologist. "One who knows himself and his passions clearly and distinctly, loves God, and that all the more, the greater this understanding is" (Sentence 15).

I am sure you are all aware that for Spinoza this third kind of knowledge, that of the wise man—that is, of the completely liberated spirit—has to be distinguished very carefully from knowledge of the second kind that does not go beyond the level of abstractions and general notions. Thus, it would be imprudent to say that Spinoza regards the sage and the scientist as strictly identical, at least not in the sense we use these words today. Spinoza undoubtedly recognized that even simple people—I mean people who possess no scientific knowledge in the strict sense of the word—can attain, if not to knowledge of the second kind, then at least to its equivalent and to true love of God.

All this, by the way, naturally brings up the serious problem of interpretation. We all know to what controversies the interpretation of Spinoza has led. But even though people generally tend to simplify complicated basic thoughts, we are nonetheless justified in seeing Spinoza as the leader of those rationalistic thinkers who, later on and even today—though their number surely has diminished—accept without reservation the claim that progress in the sciences necessarily brings with it progress in wisdom. During the Enlightenment this confidence was easy to come by, although I admit we would have to make some important distinctions. In any case, one of the crucial notions in this type of thinking is the relation of intellect and will.

In the eighteenth century, probably as early as Fénelon, especially among the English philosophers, and of course Rousseau, an entirely new conception of the moral sense and affectivity arose to combat the intellectualism of Descartes. With its appearance the significance of wisdom tended to diminish. For Goethe, because of his preference for Spinoza, wisdom retains its total preponderance, albeit with a rather strictly aristocratic flavor. The Romanticists, in my opinion, favored dissociation: on the one hand, wisdom was regarded with some disdain, and conduct was regulated by particular rules of prudence that thereby made it dependent upon reason alone, upon *ingenuity;* on the other hand, to extol wisdom, they recognized a wisdom above wisdom which belonged in the realm of intuition or, in any case, to faculties that could not be traced back to reason or to discursive thinking of any sort. Besides, there may well be a certain similarity between the Romantic conceptions and a purely Christian conception of a holy wisdom that is utter foolishness as compared with the wisdom of the world.

In any case, insofar as it did not consist solely of shrewd recommendations, wisdom seemed in no way dependent upon what might be considered positive scientific knowledge. It looks as though the more the sciences aspire to specialization, the more difficult it becomes to find a middle way between the sciences and the kind of intuitive knowledge of life closely linked with artistry and the art of living that might still deserve the honorable name of wisdom. It looks somewhat as if each science, taken singly, were trying to barricade itself against the temptation to come to grips with human existence; and here I use the notion "existence" in its present meaning and insofar as it is bound up with definite or indefinite values.

The success of the assorted theories of evolution, moreover, contributed considerably to the substitution of a biological notion for what was previously called wisdom; that is, the idea of the adaptation of man, which essentially considers him as living in a sphere of activity rather than as a thinking person. However, this only represents a very schematic formulation of thoughts that are much more complicated. The philosophers who favored the theory of evolution, naturally and with quite varied success, tried to incorporate selected elements of earlier doctrines into their theories. For example, Nietzsche and Bergson produced philosophies of life which are much richer than any previous attempts to do the same thing. The moment life is regarded as creation, it is man's business to participate actively in the creative process, even if only because his milieu is no longer considered a firmly established value, but rather is recognized as something that can be renewed and altered. This necessarily precipitates a genuinely radical change in the concept of wisdom.

Nietzsche's thought passed through astonishing variations; consequently, if we are going to study it, we will have to do so with proper regard for the different periods of his life. On the one hand we have to distinguish between his critical evaluations of behavior—which, with the addition of a few original elements, simply develop the considerations of the French moralists from La Rochefoucauld to Chamfort—and the emergence from Zarathustra onward of the prophetic view with its emphasis on everlasting return and the creation of the superman. In this latter period, thought conceivably ventures into domains that are far beyond what was traditionally implicated in the notion of wisdom. And while Bergson's thought was doubtless quite different, it too eventually became absorbed to some degree in a religious reality that was not apparent in his early writings, and which patently goes far beyond the traditional concept to which the moralists had been appealing.

After this almost offensively succinct allusion on my part, it is time to get at the problem I formulated in my preliminary remarks. I intend to treat it from an essentially phenomenological standpoint.

In my opinion, we must first listen attentively and then evalu-

ate what the word wisdom means to the majority of our fellowmen, and I am now thinking primarily of the younger generation. I think we will have to say that the first reaction to the expression "wisdom" is one of general mistrust. Why? Because it
appears to concede a primacy to experience and, to a certain extent, age. The very word has an old, musty odor about it. And
youth is apt to contest or even reject the primacy because they
hold the older generation responsible for the tragic and perhaps desperate situation in which we today find ourselves. They
might express themselves like this: There is only one possibility.
Either wisdom, as you call it, actually had a hand in the course
of events, and then it is tantamount to the worst kind of mad-
ness, or the world has developed as we find it today *in spite of* all
wise advice, and then, willy-nilly, we have to conclude that wisdom was ineffective or non-existent; at most it enabled a few
favorites to create some degree of moral comfort for themselves
that we nowadays regard with pronounced suspicion.

That is not all. Someone will probably say that wisdom in all
its known forms invariably implies an approval of the world,
or even of the social order, or at very least it implies a certain
resignation on our part, and consequently it always runs the risk
of making itself an accomplice of the worst sort of conservatism.
The conclusion of these indictments is the same: Wisdom is in
the dangerous position of ultimately becoming nothing but degenerate, and to some extent depraved, life.

Can we not meet these objections by pointing out that they
imply a notion of wisdom that is much too narrow, and that it is
precisely our business to find out if this conception cannot be ex-
panded? Doubtless the answer will be that it is at once quite easy
and particularly dangerous to give the same name to profoundly
divergent patterns of conduct, even though they may not be in
any way opposed to one another.

But before we pursue this any further, we first have to concern ourselves much more directly than we have so far with the
crucial relationship between science and wisdom. We have to
use the word "science," like that of "wisdom," with consummate
discretion.

If there is an area in which the distinction devised by Blondel between *pensée pensante* (thinking thought) and *pensée pensée* (thought thought) has to be applied, it is surely that of science. In my estimation it belongs to the nature of the scholar to remain on the level of *pensée pensante*, while the publicist or the scientist works exclusively on the level of *pensée pensée*, that is, on the level of data which he too often wants to make absolute by tearing them out of the context in which they were obtained. I spoke with a young, highly qualified scientist a few days ago, and he said that the layman has no idea of the important role played by approximation, even where unquestionable laws are concerned. He said that people generally believe a particular scientific experiment can be repeated as often as desired. But experience very often proves that each repetition is no more than an approximation; it seems as if science contains certain impurities we only rarely strain out entirely. But the interesting thing is that we never hear such statements from men who consider the data as absolute.

I am emphasizing this point to show that the genuine scholar is always on his guard against scientism and the temptation to determine human conduct by a theory of evolution, for example, as though this *theory* were the equivalent of a definitive discovery of truth. In France and Germany today, and surely elsewhere, too, it is not difficult to find men who are bringing to light the lacunae in the theories of evolution that were proposed in the past, along with the daring and rash claims that attended them. Louis Bounoure is just such a man; he is professor of mathematics and natural sciences in Strasbourg.

But what does this have to do with our subject? I think the connection is clear; the scholar, the researcher, speaks of the results of his labors in terms of wisdom, while outsiders all too often draw hasty and absolute conclusions from them. Let us define wisdom carefully: It is essentially a warning that does not speak absolutely in the name of an objective certainty, as does a certain old-fashioned theology or a dogmatic Marxism; rather, it speaks in the name of certain demands to which research must submit if it is to be research in the genuine sense.

So, science, considered as *pensée pensante*, it seems to me, has something in it that really belongs to the realm of wisdom, although admittedly this otherwise important conclusion does not take us very far. Some will say that the distinction is only of interest because it helps distinguish the scientist from the "counterfeiters of wisdom." But ultimately the center of our interest is man. Does that mean man in general? Personally I have always avoided the expression. I would prefer to say we are concerned with every single one of us considered existentially, that is, as underway from birth to death. On the one hand, the image of a road or way corresponds to some extent to the structure of the human essence; but on the other hand, the image is inadequate precisely because the road to be traversed is *liable* at any moment to be interrupted by death; as a traveler I have to regard the road I am embarked upon not as a goal but as a presence and a constant immanence. Even the word *liable* is quite meaningful in this context, for man is *not at all compelled* to meditate on this presence and thereby precipitate the question whether or not it is wise to imagine the possibility. And yet this very question seems to relate to what has always been called wisdom, and evidently it cannot be simply circumvented, although that, too, would be a solution of sorts.

Can science be of any help here? Its one hope would be psychology. But is psychology actually equipped to answer the question or even to grasp its significance? Of course, Americans consider it morbid to show any concern for one's own death, except to find means of postponing it as long as possible. The concept that plays a role here and is closely related to what I said before is that of *adjustment*. It is interesting, as a marginal note, to see how Spinoza's theory that the wise man does not think of death is actually degraded in our Americanized world. Instead, the wise man is replaced by the healthy man, the man who has adapted himself well and endeavors to make as much as possible out of his life. On the one hand, it is a question of finding normal satisfaction (in sports and in comfort, as well as in sexual relations), but, on the other hand, there is also a desire to fill one's place in society becomingly. To be sure there can also be room for devotion and nobility. The adjective *decent,* which undoubtedly enjoys greater vogue in England than in the United States, probably best fits this particular conception which, I think we can safely say, finds its place at the lower limit of what has always been looked upon as wisdom. But you may ask: Why at the lower limit? Because apparently everything that has to do with creation is excluded, as well as anything that belongs still more profoundly to the personal and fear-laden question without which, for many of us Europeans, a man is not wholly a man. Anyone who accepts this distorted view consults a psychoanalyst when he finds he has difficulties in "adjusting," just as one visits a specialist in stomach and bowel ailments when one is suffering from dyspepsia or constipation. The most important thing is that such a comparison can and must be made. Everything hinges either implicitly or explicitly on the idea that what was formerly called the spiritual life has now to be considered as biological functioning pure and simple that proceeds according to definite laws, like the functioning of the lungs, the heart or the liver.

These observations are very important for our present discussion. It is precisely our business to find out if science as such is responsible for this decline, or if it is the fault of a philosophy which appeals to it, and perhaps unjustifiably so. Anglo-Saxon positivism will certainly maintain that there is an unbroken continuity between science and a philosophy that denies itself an overall view of the world and of life. Our earlier remarks certainly point in a different direction; but we will take care of that later.

I began with death and the relationship that obtains between it and the subject, because the antithesis that we intend to expose is perhaps nowhere better exemplified. But we could have made our point in a variety of ways. Some years before the last war, André Malraux told me that during his stay in Moscow the scientistic optimism of his hosts irritated him no end. He showed them a recent newspaper account of a horrible streetcar accident and declared that, regardless of all social progress, the tragedy of death was still a fact. (Was there something like a dark premonition in this? In any case, Malraux's second wife lost her life in just such an accident during the German occupation of France.) He was told in Moscow that the streetcars and trains of the future would function so perfectly that no such accidents would ever occur. The incredible stupidity of such an answer needs no comment; but it is nevertheless very significant. Death is simply the normal end of a particular piece of apparatus or a machine that has served its time. It is no more tragic in the case of man than in that of any other machine. And we are told we can expect just such a "breakdown" when we resist what is normal. It is quite easy to recognize the common denominator in Russian and American thought. Both modes of thinking have a purely technological conception as their base.

The idea of love is similarly degraded; and any number of analogous facts could be adduced to prove it. Again, it threatens to reduce human reality to a single, shallow plane. As far as love, as we know it, is concerned, we have to be satisfied with distinguishing between the instinct of reproduction, on the one hand, and its gratification, on the other. This latter has to be regulated in such a way that no individual upsets the proper balance and thus by chance impairs the social contribution that he can and must make.

But this does not settle the question as to whether or not we are dealing with corollaries that derive directly from the nature of science, and this would also include scientific anthropology.

But at root everything we have said involves the basic problem of judging values.

I was disconcerted over the fact that most neo-positivistic philosophers in the United States agreed that a value judgment merely reflects an individual preference; in short, a value judgment is deceptive, and wisdom is reduced to a purely personal norm of life that does not allow itself to be generalized. This would ultimately lead us to something like a moral *diatetics*. But even diatetics implies the notion of health, whereas the kind of thought we are discussing seems to put even that into question.

However, in view of what I said earlier, we have to ask whether a science that is conscious of its potentialities to a high degree does not demand a humility that belongs to the realm of true wisdom. Let me clarify this if I may.

First, why do I put so much emphasis on humility? Because technical progress with all that it entails, seems to contain a constant provocation to boundless pride. It is almost impossible to exaggerate the significance of the heroic accomplishments of the astronauts, and, regardless of the element of personal heroism, the calculations that made their feats possible. Never before has the scriptural promise, "You will be like gods," found such striking application. But can we simply reject as false the thought that elation leads to folly, as the ancients said with such incomparable force? But one might object: Even if we admit that an individual's pride inevitably leads to some kind of mental disturbance, we are still a long way from proving that this holds true of humanity as a whole. Another objection might be: We clearly see the responsibility of the individual toward society as well as toward mankind in general, but does this dictum mean anything for humanity as such? I propose this question without reference to theology, for man's responsibility before God retains its due significance when one proceeds from Christian premises, whereas the notion of wisdom we are concerned with here belongs to the profane sphere.

I have spoken of mankind as a whole. But on consideration this global manner of speaking hardly seems to correspond to reality. While it is certainly possible to imagine the whole of humanity as nothing more than a fiction, I still perceive something genuinely contradictory to human nature in representing it as a whole. We have to get back to reality; and what do we see? A corps of international scholars who are invested with limitless power by the sum total of living men? In this case, we would have to say they are proud. The very thought of such a mandate is purely fictitious. But granting for a moment such a corps existed, we could not separate the scholars from the governments that grant them the funds they need for their purposes, nor could even the scholars themselves rightly judge their common purpose as long as the present confusion lasts between their real intentions and the principles to which they appeal. What does this all mean in terms of our theme? Just this: we would be making a grave mistake if we were to blame science itself for the disorders we have mentioned; we would be looking for responsibility where it does not at all reside.

And here a new, disquieting question appears, particularly with respect to the scholar's attitude. He might claim that his

discoveries are being utilized for purposes that he himself dis-
approves of, or for purposes that he considers disastrous for mankind. Can we be satisfied with the too convenient solution of
simply distinguishing between the man and the scholar? That
would mean that the scholar is not interested in the consequences
of his actions, while man as such himself is bound to take them
into account. I think Einstein, for example, would have repu-
diated any such separation. When he protested with pathetic
vehemence against the military use of atomic energy, he surely
did not have the feeling he was, in a sense, ignoring his role
as scholar.

I think his conception of truth is mandatory for us all. True,
we have to find a middle course between a utilitarianism or
a pragmatism that subordinates what we call truth to definite,
practical ends, and a worship of truth that sets truth up like a
Moloch of sorts to whom everything has to be sacrificed, includ-
ing the human race.

I believe that in the course of this lecture we have found, if not
the elements of a solution, at least hints that indicate where we
will have to look for it. Keep in mind what we said about the suspicious mistrust of the authentic scientist toward the simplifica-
tions of scientism. The germ of his apprehension is his research;
he wants to make its immanent conditions more and more precise, so that the problem of method will always remain open. Research itself is not amenable to hypostatization, and that is a negative but significant advantage. It cannot be separated from the
man who is actually doing the research, and thus it always remains connected with anthropology, as I hinted above. But nowadays we generally understand research to mean researching
with others, and this implies at least a minimum of mutual goodwill. Research implies a disposition that lies along the line of
peace and, as it were, on the threshold of love.

This is still no reason for us to close our eyes to certain disturbing realities. Think of the experiments that numerous Nazi
doctors made with live prisoners. And, unfortunately, we are
not at all sure that other doctors elsewhere under different and
still unimaginable circumstances may not succumb to the identical temptation to make use of human merchandise that other

tyrants may make available. In any case, being a researcher does not exclude these frightful and sinister possibilities; on the contrary, it may even encourage them in certain cases. Perhaps we can console ourselves somewhat with the fact that *at least in the world of today* scientists unanimously foreswear such aberrations, but note: I expressly said "in the world of today." We have no idea what will happen tomorrow. The population development might possibly lead to a radical degradation of, and disregard for, human existence; the latter could become so devaluated that people might consider it superfluous to surround it with the precautionary measures and the respect it now enjoys. In fact, it is even conceivable that respect and precautionary measures would then contradict what we today regard as healthy human understanding.

Here we meet another problem whose data clearly illustrate the perplexing situation facing modern man when he investigates the connections between science and wisdom, namely, the problem of birth rates and the resulting overpopulation of the earth. In view of the unceasing difficulties which the rapid population increase threatens to bring with it, is not the scientist warranted in submitting personal recommendations he believes have been inspired by wisdom? And if he is so warranted what is likely to happen to the distinction between science and wisdom? Will it vanish? At first sight this looks like an admirable question. This much is clear: Science must apply itself to the problem and endeavor to solve it in its original sphere. That means it must strive to assure the sustenance of the ever-increasing population with every possible means. But would science not be overstepping its rights if it ventured into the area of private life; would not the scientist then be usurping an office that in no way belongs to him? Here again, we have to be very specific. At this very moment—I am speaking now of us in the West—we would find it intolerable if the right to procreate, which rests with individual couples, were suddenly to be regulated by some international organization. And what of our "senior citizens" who have ceased to be productive—how are they to be kept alive, as they must be? It is quite conceivable that as the process of desacralization continues and accelerates we can expect that tomorrow all the restraints still standing today will be razed. This is a matter of technocratic development in itself, and the outcome will be the same, whether it happens in an American or a Soviet world.

Again we have to ask whether it is really science as such that we ought to indict. I feel that before we can answer some very fine distinctions are in order. There can be no doubt that science, with the power it exercises not only over nature but also over people, is partially responsible for leading men into temptation. On the other hand, it is extremely questionable whether science actually promotes the means or inner sources of self-help which will enable man to withstand the temptation. You see, we are not about to get away from what I said about the scientist himself and the humility required for every kind of research worthy of the name; but it is obvious that what I said in no way applies to the would-be scientist, that is, to the innumerable people who profit from the work of authentic scientists and give others the benefit of it. Anyway, on this level absolutely nothing is guaranteed. I have often said previously that technical skills can easily become dangerous when they are no longer engaged in serving metatechnical ends. And while science may not disavow these ends outright, I fear it tends to simply ignore them. The dangerous possibility exists that the applied sciences—in Europe as well as America—will emphasize goals that occupy a place of inferior importance among the values determined by wise men of the past. Naturally, a number of problems flow together at this point. It can always be objected that a particular order of precedence makes sense only in an aristocratic milieu, and consequently it cannot exist in the world of the masses now taking shape before our very eyes. But I personally feel that such an answer taken literally, implies something very much like an approval of the degradation of the human race. Really, it all depends on what we understand by aristocracy. Can we be satisfied with a universal leveling coming from below? Can we deny that precisely among the masses new aristocracies have to be formed that obviously can no longer be based on race or money? Be that as it may, I am still convinced science can never justify this radical leveling, which as Nietzsche and Scheler have definitely proven, is rooted in resentment. Perhaps before concluding it would be advisable at this point to recall what has stood out in the course of our meanderings.

In the first place, I feel I have to insist on the basic distinction between wisdom and the sort of generalized hygiene to which certain technocratically oriented minds would like to reduce it. It is basically a problem of tracing the common root of *justesse* and *justice*, of precision and justice. I should like to express this in terms of music and say that perhaps wisdom is the strict maintenance of a certain keynote, such as one finds in Marcus Aurelius, Socrates, Goethe and Spinoza. It may be difficult to define the tone without sacrificing its value. I like to call it an essence: and essence is not a definite, objectifiable content, but rather a certain kind of light, and it is a joy to be light. That leads us to the point I have been circling for some time now. For is not ultimately the genuine joy of the scholar whose research is succeeding and progressing only an expression of this joy? Perhaps we should see in the *gaudium cognoscendi* (the joy of knowing), and to a certain extent a foretaste of the *laetitia contemplandi* (the joy of contemplating), the final and highest purpose of our earthly pilgrimage.

There is no such thing as atonal wisdom, I dare say; nor can there be. Atonality in life is disorder and aberration. But wisdom is, finally, perhaps the joyful effort to conquer and master ignorance and fear, just as science on its part is a victory over illusions. So, perhaps here at the end of our investigation we can notice a certain convergence between the two notions.

Wisdom is to be found wherever man tries not to organize his life around a center; instead he strives to organize it with respect to everything that has to do with the business of keeping oneself in existence; all else he regards as peripheral and subordinate.

But science for its part is simply a heap of scattered cognitions, unless it establishes itself around a center. We have to say here that this center remains much more heavily veiled than is the case on the level of personal life. Perhaps here lie the roots of our difficulties.

I have, incidentally, also given you to understand that if one speaks about wisdom in a self-confident tone, one will probably bring to light even the spirit of science, which is actually research. Naturally, we have to add at once that we hardly carry on research merely for the pleasure it affords. Perhaps we ought to say that we labor to gain possession of the world interiorly, as far as possible. But because "assimilating the world" can also mean attempting to own it, or to do as we please with it, we are going to have to deal with a deviation that may occur at any time and can cause the actual and pure intention of the scholar to be dangerously spoiled. It is my conviction that appropriating to oneself interiorly can be understood in a quite different sense, that is, in the same sense in which we try to appropriate a poem or a piece of music interiorly. This does not necessarily mean that we could also play the music or recite the poem. Rather, it means realizing a definite consonance, a definite harmony with the world, but not through expedients that are bound up with loose imagination; on the contrary, our method has to be very exact.

But how is it that the scholar only very seldom seems to be conscious of this goal? Perhaps it is because, mentally, he is concentrating so strongly on the means and is constantly perfecting and polishing them that eventually he is incapable of fixing his eye upon a goal that cannot be formulated in the language of his means. Perhaps the role of philosophy is, in part, to make just such understanding available to the scholar, to bring to his ear the "keynote" we mentioned, and thus, in some measure, to negotiate between science and a wisdom that continues to be active in our lives despite those who would scorn it. Wisdom appears estranged from the world of the spirit only because we have fallen into the deplorable habit of representing it to ourselves according to the criterion of currently popular literature and philosophies. If we want to approach the mysterious precincts in which science and wisdom converge without losing their individual identities, we will first have to dismantle the barriers that obstruct authentic understanding.

III

The Sacral in the
Era of Technology

We are now about to turn our attention to one of the gravest problems of our day and age. If we are willing to eschew the narrowly religious perspective and recognize the problem in its rightful proportions, it looms as what might well be the most crucial problem facing man today—the believer and non-believer alike. For in effect it poses the question: What are we to make of ourselves in face of the fact that we are gradually being thoroughly manipulated by a technology that we ourselves have devised?

First of all, we will have to define the relevant notions with added precision. And it is only fitting that we begin by distinguishing between the sacral and the holy. This becomes more necessary owing to the fact that in German we are apt to confuse the two, as the word *heilig* can be used for either notion. In English the word *holy,* as well as the word *saint,* can be defined with relatively greater ease. For instance, I can appeal to what Paul Tillich says in the first volume of his *Systematic Theology*: "The sphere of the gods is the sphere of holiness. A sacred realm is established wherever the divine is manifested. Whatever is brought into the divine sphere is consecrated. The divine is the holy."

In this sense one might assert that God alone is holy, and that holiness (*sanctitas*) belongs to him, and him alone. Consequently when we refer to someone as a saint, our reference is only true to the extent he appears to participate in the holiness of God. With this in mind one might well ask whether Tillich really has a right to say that holiness is something we can experience and something that lends itself to phenomenological description. Here we touch on a rather difficult point, but we need not go into it at the moment. Tillich, in his peculiar fashion, would say that the holy is that particular quality of whatever concerns man ultimately; it alone can give man ultimate meaning and vice versa.

Without going into a rigorous analysis, it already seems clear enough that when we talk about the holy we are attending to something that is extremely nebulous. Furthermore, philosophical investigation might well go to show that this something is apparently related to holiness, that is to say, to the holiness of God. But this is far from being self-evident, and in my estimation we should meditate on what it actually means to experience the sacral, and how it is that even non-believers, or, more precisely, people who do not regard themselves believers, can also experience it. I personally would study the act of experience precisely insofar as it affects modern man, namely, man belonging as he does to the transitional world in which we presently live. Up to now we have lived in a world with certain definite values, but at the moment we are facing a different world altogether—one still in its inaugural stages, where the values of yesterday are going to be questioned radically, if not denied or rejected outright. This situation, cloven as it is, will be the basis of everything to come; the world we are now living in is, if I may say so, essentially one of transition. As so often in the past, I shall in this essay assume my own peculiar form of meditating, for I, too, have to realize that I am a rent individual in the process of transition.

What do I mean when I say the people around me have entered the era of technology? I certainly want to do more than simply reiterate that in recent times technology has made remarkable progress. What I particularly want to stress is man's growing tendency to understand the world around him—and even himself—in terms of technology. But then of course, I should specify what I mean by technology. I consider it a specialized and rationally elaborated skill that can be improved and taught to others. When we speak of technology we do not have in mind the cumulative sum of a variety of different skills. Technology is not a unity we can amass. It is human reason insofar as it strives to manage, so to speak, the earth and everything living within it. Today it might even extend to the management of other planets, although this is still only a possibility, and no one really knows whether it is destined to become reality or not.

To maintain as I do that man is being misled to understand the world and himself in reference to technology, postulates that man is under the impression he can modify the world methodically by his own industry in such a way as to satisfy his needs in an increasingly perfect manner. Some time ago I called attention to the fact that this kind of thinking gives rise to a genuine anthropocentrism. Man tends to look upon himself as alone being capable of giving meaning to an otherwise meaningless world. Doubtless this will have a remarkable effect on man's ability to admire the things around him; there will be an increased tendency to admire the products of his own technology—as they appear to afford a matchless measure of perfection and precision. The German critic Günther Anders, in an outstanding book published some time ago entitled *Die Antiquiertheit des Menschen* (The Antiquatedness of Man), tried to show how eventually man will see himself as something of a nuisance, almost refuse, for being nothing more than human. And then he will set about rectifying the evident shortcomings in what he understands by "nature."

We could adduce countless examples, but I would like to mention contraceptive devices in particular, as they seem about to assure man of mastery over a function to which he was formerly so blindly subject as to lead many progressive spirits to judge it to be actually contrary to the genuine best interests of the race and of the individual. Since I am not about to debate the desirability of such mastery, I will simply say that from a technocratic point of view it can be nothing but desirable. But this presumes an assumption which we have a perfect right to put into question. I shall have to return to this point further on.

These, and similar reasons that do not come to mind at the moment, seem to favor this particular kind of thinking. Are not the most enlightened spirits of our age intent upon organizing the earth as scientifically as possible? Would we be able to alleviate the hunger of the world, for instance, if this enterprise should fail? Obviously *not;* for the solution first and foremost entails the distribution of raw materials and disclosing the world's vast larder of untouched resources. A major problem like that of developing entire nations can be solved only with the assistance of technological progress. Again, we could cite any number of examples, and they could only be denied by unprogressive spirits who are amateurish in their thinking and hardly comprehend the imminent danger of the situation. In fact it seems that we have gotten to the point where we are faced with a categorical necessity we cannot avoid without regressing to a state of unparalleled barbarity.

By and large, the characteristic attitude of technocratic thinking does not consist solely in propounding the principles we elucidated above, but also in considering as somehow futile *everything* that would obstruct the forward movement of technology. Precisely this latter attitude conjures up the problem I would like to consider at length. Again it is in reference to the development of contraceptives.

We simply have to understand the opposition of many faithful believers, especially Catholics, to their general use. The employment of such devices seems to imply a misunderstanding, if not an outright denial, of the sacred character of life. For reasons we ought to be aware of, believers see procreation as something very much more than a purely biological function. Even the word "procreation" would seem out of place in this context insofar as it intimates a *process* of generating life that actually degrades the act of propagation to some extent; it does away with that very element which, in the eyes of the believer, gives it its particular value as well as its transcendence. Naturally, the biologist has no other alternative but to call this value and transcendence into question; he finds it foolish to draw a distinction of nature between conception and any other physiological process. But what is particularly—if not solely—important is the fact that a husband and wife as procreators are limited to fulfilling the conditions according to which a human being, an image of God, becomes flesh. It is extremely important to realize that this entails a gift of God; and man has to place himself in God's service. If we proceed from the acknowledgment of this gift, and from this acknowledgment alone, it definitely is possible to attribute a sacral character to life. The indiscriminate manipulation of human life, on the other hand, to which any kind of contraceptive practice might lead, would seem to imply a disregard for the fact that the power of procreation is a gift. Man tends to function as though he were the actual producer and not merely a mediating agent. Furthermore, mediation is closely associated with the act of producing; in fact every activity looked upon by man as creative actually has to be understood as mediative.

Therefore, I think everyone will agree that because of scientific and technological progress, man has come to look upon himself as a creator rather than an agent. And I will admit that in a world that is (or is becoming) ours everything is apparently proceeding as though this substitution were sanctioned by reason. Consequently, we will have to make a strenuous effort if we are going to extricate ourselves and restore the forgotten reality of mediation.

Doubtless others will think we are foolish. After all, as they see it, it means swimming against the inexorable tide of progress. In other words we are being asked to reject our rather "theocentric" explanation of reproduction and be courageous enough to acknowledge that the reproductive act is no one's business but man's.

While we are on the subject of reproduction, it should be obvious enough that the industrial notion of reproduction hardly fits into our present context. Procreation is not the same thing as fabrication. The seed, or more precisely the semen, transmits a past that is literally unbounded. Consequently man can never be wholly conscious of what he is about when performing the procreative act; the full implications of the deed infinitely exceed his powers of consciousness. In effect he is implementing a procedure he cannot possibly explain. This is just the opposite of what happens in the industrial process, where the materials are not only completely understandable, but actually have to be understood if the process is to meet with any success. No one will object, I am sure—as Heidegger seems to have clearly foreseen as a possibility—that in its peculiar way technology is an heir of idealism. The act by which life is transmitted goes on in opposition not only to the "I think," the *"cogito,"* but to all purely rational thought, because it is fundamentally inscrutable.

Several questions are in order: Is it not completely arbitrary to interpret this obscurity as indicating some form of the sacral? Would it not be more normal simply to regard it as witnessing to the fact that man, rooted as he is in a darkened nature, has to consider that he is called to liberate himself as far as possible and eventually gain access to the light of reason?

Actually I hardly think we can dismiss this objection or even substantially modify it; but if such a thing is possible, I think it will have to be reached by way of a very long and circuitous route and on condition that the sacral be regarded as transcending experience. In other words, even granting that someday we might be able, with the help of paleontological discoveries, to go back in time to what we call our origin, this would still not provide us with any substantial illumination, for the further we penetrate into pre-history, the more faint our understanding becomes. This is not to say that our origin cannot be illuminated at all, but if it is to be illuminated the light will have to come from some other quarter.

We have to keep in mind that there is a fundamental difference between production and propagation: the begetter is essentially a go-between between the past and the future, both of which elude him. But to the measure we approach our debut into the world, it becomes possible to locate a point where the sacral has its proper place—as exemplified, perhaps, by those religions that practice ancestor worship.

But without undertaking a purely sociological investigation, we have to become aware of the intimate contact that obtains within the family. I tried to point it out in my *Homo Viator,* where I wrote:

When I speak of the family I conjure up, on the one hand, a definite image, a specific constellation, and think it is self-evident that I, the child, am the center of it. Am I not the object of a care that at one time touches me tenderly, at another time oppresses me and becomes burdensome—a care whose every nuance affects me because all those around me betray intentions that seem to be pointed at my person? The same is true of the inflection in their voices when they speak; there is an entire register of meaning, from mildness to sternness, from persuasion to threat. Only gradually do I distinguish the relationships that bind these beings to each other. And so I gradually discern that each of them has his own life, his sacrosanct relationships with all the others, and that for some of them I am an object of their solicitude and a subject of conversation when I am not among them. The thoughts and feelings I arouse in these people who invariably show me the same face—these I come to know only in a form altered to suit my use.

From this moment on, everything becomes strangely complicated. New relationships arise between them and me; when I notice that they hide from me, how can I escape the temptation to hide myself from them? But at the same time, strange contours appear in my personal life, and it closes in upon itself. The simple and undisturbed landscape of my early years becomes more complicated and overcast. My family keeps away from me but stays nevertheless as near as possible, and I do the same to them. It would be difficult to imagine another tear-wound that would be harder to heal. But that is not all; in fact it is hardly the beginning. Imperceptibly, I discover beneath the abstract words fatherhood and sonship hidden and forbidden realities that make my soul dizzy. They lure me on; but I turn away from them because I think it would be a sacrilege to yield to their enticements. At least I shall understand that I am in no way provided with absolute existence; rather, I *am*, without having either willed or suspected that I represent *embodiment* as an answer to the double call that two beings have issued to each other in the unknown, no doubt directed to an incomprehensible power above themselves that expresses itself by giving life. I *am* this at-first formless answer; only gradually and to the extent that I develop, will I recognize myself as answer and as judgment. Indeed, I am unavoidably led to the discovery that I am, solely by the fact that I am the being that I am, a judgment upon those who brought me into existence; thus arises an infinity of new relations between them and myself.

Then I affirmed the impenetrable darkness enveloping what I called the stream of my forebears and the limitless net of antecedents, a net that could ultimately be coextensive with the human race.

All that I am able to recognize in this growing and overpowering indefiniteness is the fact that these unknown beings that push themselves between me and the inconceivable sources of whatever kind are not simple causes whose effect or offspring I am. Concepts like cause and effect doubtless lose their significance here; between my ancestors and me there must exist an infinitely more obscure and more intimate relationship: I have a share in them, as they have in me—in the invisible; they are to me, and I to them, consubstantial.

Therefore, my intention was to show that a certain form of the sacral, offering itself as a salutary veil, can be present in the compact reality of the family.

The objection we can expect—and that which points up quite vividly the fundamental problem—goes as follows: Nowadays it appears that the family, far from being anything like a salutary protection, represents a confusing network of hindrances, with man trying desperately to extricate himself. I perhaps would even go a bit further and say that it looks like the work is being done for him. For sociology tells us that the family is diminishing in size, not only by reason of the diminishing number of parents and children, but, more significantly, because paternal authority is being ever more gravely challenged and, of all things, precisely by those who ought to exercise it. In another chapter of *Homo Viator* I have tried to show that the true sense of fatherhood is not biological; it has to do with a particular vocation. But this vocation itself presupposes regard for life. It includes the corollary (of which we are perhaps all too unaware) that the words "to impart life," have to be interpreted in their truest sense, namely, that life is an infinitely precious gift, and that the father himself is only a mediator between God as the author of all creation and the child as a creature of God.

But precisely this fact reveals the process of desacralization. Today life is rarely thought of as a benefaction. People are more

inclined to underscore what life implies in the way of revealing
absurdity and precipitating despair. Hence, parents look upon
themselves as having unjustifiably destined someone who did
not ask for life to share the same unintelligible and too often
disastrous gamble in which they themselves are implicated.
Philosophically speaking, this is the most important aspect of the
problem we dealt with a moment ago in our discussion of contra-
ception. If we proceed from a completely desacralized, pessimistic view of life we tend to treat life simply as a power we have to
control if we are going to minimize its baneful effects. But in effect this pessimistic outlook is a definite component of the technological notion of the world. It leads us to arrogate to itself the
right to manipulate life—simply because it has none of those
sacral qualities we discover through a theocentric perspective.

It would be similarly fitting to meditate on man's conduct in
the face of death. I am speaking, of course, about the death of
someone else, not one's own. For a long time it was noticeable in
France how people preserved their respect for death long after
their own personal faith had disappeared. But now I think we
have a right to ask if even this respect is about to disappear, and,
if so, can we attribute its disappearance to any particular kind of
thinking. It would seem that life is regarded as entirely useless;
consequently, one can extinguish it like a candle. Murder is
gradually losing that stigma proper to it in light of the Ten Com-
mandments; we hardly recognize it as a crime anymore. Doubtless we can trace the trend to the terrible mass murders that were
perpetrated during the two World Wars and the pogroms. But
what I particularly have in mind is the statistical presentation
of the facts that ultimately and unnoticeably infects those who
have never killed and who doubtless remain true to the traditional view on the subject in their manner of judging. I am almost tempted to speak in stock market jargon about a devastating
"drop" in the price of life. Here as anywhere else in business life
numbers have an important function. But the number factor
operates in absolute opposition to the sacral. The very act of
counting itself, I would think, is the beginning of desecration.
And if this is so, it is all the more true of statistical evaluation,
though, admittedly, those entrusted with the preservation of gen-

uine religious values often condescend to this kind of reckoning—just so much more proof of how far along the process of desacralization actually is. And, conversely, it perhaps helps us grasp the true essence of the sacral *in itself.*

This is an opportune moment for me to refer to some of my earlier writings. In notes I wrote in 1930 on the prevailing lack of religion, I pointed out that the feeling for the sacral belongs to a realm where the subject finds himself face to face with something beyond his comprehension. Nothing, I said at the time, is more characteristic than the behavior of the believer who folds his hands and by this very gesture declares that there is nothing to be done and nothing to be changed; he simply resigns himself. His gesture is one of dedication and worship.

But conceivably I have still not made the case for the inviolability of the sacral plainly enough. I want to show it to be there where we face whatever is in itself defenseless. For a person who has not been totally absorbed by the technical and, let us say, dehumanized world, contemplation of the most frail of creatures is better suited than anything else to incite him to adoration. Think of the toddler when he suddenly ceases to be a squirming something and his face lights up in a smile. The very presence of the defenseless creature disarms us of all the instruments that would have enabled us to take the actualities in hand and alter them. In my opinion we can best understand "transcendence" within this framework. But it is equally certain that what we have said will be branded as sickly, and perhaps even disastrous, sentimentality by those who look upon themselves as the shock troops of the latest forms of technology—in particular psychoanalysis, at least when it adheres to a naturalistic philosophy (as seems true in the case of Freud, in his earliest writings at least). The psychoanalyst will no doubt cede us the right, though grudgingly, to be touched by the little child; but he will generally deny that the compassion involved—if we may call it that—has anything to do with truth. Now, this is important, for the word *sacral* ceases to have any meaning; as soon as one ceases to accept that it refers to an actuality that absolutely transcends the level of simple emotion, it degenerates into a nondescript epithet. Moreover, if we were to emphasize in the sacral that element which can in no way be attributed to states of consciousness and still less to kinds of behavior, we would certainly be led to discover the hidden, intimate relationship between the sacral and holiness in which connection I cited Tillich at the beginning of this lecture. It is not impossible that the sacral, on condition it retains its full meaning, has its foundation in a conviction concerning the holiness of God. And, conversely, I feel it is extremely probable that once we impugn this conviction in the name of a "theodicy in reverse," so to speak, we will eventually do away with the sacral altogether.

We are now in a position to recognize that in a world where technology enjoys absolute primacy, a desacralizing process inevitably sets in that is directed against life and all its manifestations, and particularly against the family and everything connected with it. On the other hand, experience indicates that in totalitarian countries, at least, a strongly nationalized society is attempting to take over and reinstate precisely those elements the family has lost—and that to their own advantage. But we also know that this only leads to the formation of nothing more than the "pseudo-sacral." This is destined to arouse criticism, and a totalitarian society can only defend itself by having recourse to force, coercion and terror.

There are those who would reject both alternatives: the sacral that is only a relic of the past and which depends on a *Weltanschauung* sufficiently refuted by science, as well as the "pseudo-sacral" that is introduced by tyrannical governments at the expense of the individual's right to mold his own conscience. In their stead they would propose that the world be based on contractual, that is to say, voluntarily approved, relationships; a democracy worthy of the name is actually nothing else. While their attitude appears reasonable enough, I fear it reflects a profound ignorance of the authentic human condition. Agreement, by its very nature, requires an oath, that is to say, the sacral. But at the same time experience clearly proves that a contract actually tends to desacralize itself and eventually degenerates into an agreement that each party tries to use to his own best advantage. Or it may simply become a bureaucratic adjustment that no one actually observes; instead everyone tries to circumvent it as far as possible. This malignancy—the core of bureaucracy almost everywhere—is only possible on the basis of the kind of degradation we described above, and it is very difficult, if not impossible, to see how it can be avoided. At best we can try to gloss it over. But how can we overlook the fact that there is a reverse side to the phenomenon: human profiteering is growing more and more complicated, and to the extent I exert myself to discover solutions for the countless practical problems resulting from and posed by numbers, I will have recourse to the domain of statistics. And I find it extremely difficult to believe that statistics can at all be sacral, for they postulate a lack of consideration for, or implicit indifference to, the individual. The only way to rediscover the path to the sacral is to turn away from the world and recapture simplicity, which is perhaps only another word for uniqueness and inwardness, *the favorite abode of the sacral.*

It is vain to hope that human reality as it is comprehended by statistical methods could ever admit the sacral. It is completely foreign to grace. Grace can only reach the individual, and if it reaches the masses through the individual then it will only happen if the masses arouse themselves from the stupor that made them masses in the first place. I have in mind certain events we look upon as miraculous, Fatima, for example. Although I am not about to underrate the infinitely complex and difficult problems arising from apparitions of that kind, even the most religious of men should not accept them without some caution, without of course refusing to believe—for that would simply be rash.

All these considerations lead to a single conclusion: in the technical era the sacral can only reveal itself on condition we are converted (taking of course the word *conversion* in its usual sense). It seems unreasonable to presume the sacral will ever reveal itself of a sudden in the sweep of development that we constantly have before our eyes. On the contrary, the development itself is aimed at a general and fundamental rejection of the sacral, and this to the degree it encourages ever more explicitly a Promethean attitude—with its attendant hubris, or pride.

But what exactly do we mean by conversion? I do not think we should place the emphasis on one's particular religious confession, although admittedly conversion does usually have a con-

fessional character. But the very least we can say is that conversion can reveal itself in different ways. Conversion is first of all
the movement by which the consciousness turns away from the
oppressive and distressing spectacle that the technocratic view of
the world offers, or—and this amounts to the same thing—by
which consciousness transcends the obsession with numbers
through the numberless. It is the inwardness we regain through
an action which is not only free, but in fact is freedom *itself*. But
we have to remember that in its essence inwardness is not tantamount to restriction, and it would be gravely deceptive to think
so. And it is just as wrong to imagine the individual who becomes
a unity all to himself on account of his conversion. The exact opposite is true; inwardness must be reciprocal; it is a relationship of one individual to another, of an "I" to a "Thou," as both
Martin Buber and I have tried to prove in our writings.

IV
Death and
Immortality

In first outlining the scope of this lecture I would like to make it clear that I am not going to speak about death and immortality as a theologian. But, then, it is not at all certain that the notion of immortality as such comes within the scope of theology; whereas, I admit, the resurrection certainly does. So, I shall speak as a philosopher, and indeed, I should like to add, as a philosopher of reflection.

It would appear that very many people have failed to recognize the connections that exist between my thinking and that of the French philosophy of the nineteenth century, and particularly my debt to Maine de Biran and those who carried on his work. The only philosopher, to my knowledge, who has presented this association clearly is a Scotsman, Jan Alexander, who wrote a very noteworthy work on my philosophy some ten or fifteen years ago. Unfortunately no publisher in Great Britain would venture to publish his comprehensive work, even though it earned for its author a doctor's degree, and that with the most splendid commendations.

If I am insisting on the reflective character of my thinking, it is because I want to emphasize at the outset that no one should expect from me arbitrary, fantastic speculations about the life to

come and its mysterious character. But I, too, think it is fundamentally significant, and I hope to present it in a clear enough
fashion so that the mystery involved will be acknowledged for its
illuminating and liberating merits. I believe unreservedly that
many of the dreadful evils besetting mankind—among them
some of the most pernicious perversions we will find—are intimately associated with the general haziness surrounding just this
mystery. I feel it concerns us vitally, and for this reason it deserves to be better understood.

This mystery is of such a nature that its rejection deprives human life not only of its principal dimension, but also, little by
little, of its entire significance and depth. This is still no reason
why I should go ahead and approve this or that spiritualistic,
theosophic view, though some people have pretended—without
the least plausible reason, I might add—to regard me as an ad-
vocate of such views. Now, it is true I occupy an extremely subtle
position on this question, and I hope in the concluding section
of this lecture to make it clear just how far I am willing to go in
this direction. But I will likewise clearly specify the bounds I am
unwilling to overstep.

The question I would like to raise is this: What is my attitude
toward death, or, more precisely, what is my attitude toward my
own death? You see, I do not want to deliver a lecture; instead I
would like to meditate aloud.

I no sooner posed the question, than I realized just how ambiguous it actually is. Are we trying to find out how "I," the man
whose name is in the public registry office, and who is endowed
with the empirical individuality proper to *me* and is at that precise point in time that *I* have reached on the way from birth and
death—how "I," this man, regard my own death? Upon consideration we are bound to see how ambiguous this mode of expression
is.

What does it mean to "assume an attitude"? Even the French
expression *se situer*, being reflexive, is no less confusing in this
context. What is meant by the "strictly subjective reaction to
the thought of one's own death"? Does it show whether I actually
fear death, or for that matter await it in full confidence although
I hardly look forward to it as a deliverance? Does that mean I re-

gard death with indifference? While all this might be interesting enough psychologically, it is not at all what I wanted to say with what turns out to be an unfortunate choice of words.

Above all, then, and at least for the time being, the subject (myself) or the one questioning (himself) has to be divested of his particular character, his individuality. The "I" has to be "departicularized," if you will excuse the expression. But that is precisely the problem; can I carry this departicularizing to the extreme where "I" becomes a sort of Kantian or Fichtean transcendental Ego that sets about examining itself in my person? Evidently we are not going to be able to consider this possibility here.

The "I" (je) that ponders thoughts about its own death is not, nor can it be, a pure abstraction like the transcendental "I" (moi). Consequently, one cannot take seriously the idealistic attempt to rescue immortality by asserting that the thinking subject, of its very nature, cannot die. For actually, to begin with, such a subject cannot even live. I would prefer to leave such imagings to the antiquated philosophy that originated them. If this idea has any value at all, it would be only in epistemology, or the study of cognition, and then only if one is willing to assume that it can be entirely separated from a specific, concrete philosophy; and I am not at all sure that it can.

These reflections lead us to an important observation: The departicularization we are speaking of can only occur partially. The man who asks is a man among other men. He is related to a specific situation that all human beings have in common. This leaves the question open as to whether or not there are other beings who perhaps are not subject to mortality, to death.

That I must die, that death is a law for all men, I can know by *induction;* but I could just as well *deduce* it from the character of this organic body of mine. Yet all this belongs to the realm of knowledge: I know, I have learned, that I shall die. Still, it could also be—but this is somewhat doubtful—that I bear death within me as a presentiment, with or without any sort of knowledge. But I think one has to admit that this foreboding, or this foreknowledge, enters my consciousness only at certain moments or perhaps at a certain period of life. At other times, on the contrary, I might even possess the clear consciousness, whether I imagine it or not, that I shall not have to die, indeed, that I cannot die. In themselves, however, these are accidental experiences or "cognitions" that we cannot properly evaluate.

I spoke of an organized body. But is this certainty, referring as it does to an object and hence being objective, an existential certainty that applies to the "I" that is at this very moment posing the question? We see at once that this is extremely obscure. When I say: I know that death is in store for me at some point in the future, it is not the same as saying: "My body will cease to perform its functions and disintegrate." Such an induction, it seems to me, would falsify the radical nature of my certainty that I must die. It would be equally inexact to claim to know that I will not, or cannot, survive the dissolution of my body. To appeal to knowledge here would be to invoke something like a dogmatic declaration that is neither granted, nor could be granted, to my meditative consciousness. Furthermore, we have to prescind from what I as this or that individual, perhaps as a believer, personally think about the matter. But obviously, it would not be less unreasonable to insist upon a dogmatic declaration of the opposite kind—one that would amount to a dualism between my body and me. Perhaps it would be fairly accurate to say that this being-destined-to-die involves an encounter with some kind of unknown something; but this "something" represents an end or an absolute limit, if one considers it from the viewpoint of earthly life, insofar as the latter is involved with obligations and potentialities.

You may perhaps be surprised that I express myself so vaguely. But in this case every exact designation would be arbitrary, as for example the use of the word "occurrence." My death, you see, appears less as something that will "happen to me" than something that makes every other event impossible, at least in the view I mentioned. On the other hand, the word "encounter" is extremely important, since it at least admits the possibility of my assuming an attitude toward my impending death and behaving in this or that manner toward it. I am using the word "possibility" tentatively and only in a negative sense: It is not impossible that I might remain unmoved, so to speak, regarding my death, without either intending or being aware of laziness. By no means, then, does my laziness in this case deserve to be called an "attitude." However, I will admit that after reflecting long enough I probably will realize that I have to take some position. In doing so I make use of my freedom; but it is a freedom that is able to suspend itself.

At this point, I want to develop a line of thought I introduced in my lecture at the International Philosophy Convention held in Paris in 1937; I think I ought to read at least a paragraph of this lecture to you:

> In spite of the clouds that veil the future, that is, *my* future, it remains unalterably certain that I shall die. Of all the things that await me, only my death is certain. My death is not yet a fact. Is it an idea, then? If it were an idea, it would have to be possible for me to get rid of it, but I cannot. I can only accept it and consider it an actuality, if I put myself in the place of someone else who outlives me, and who, referring to what I call "my death," says "his death. . . ." In reality, however, this certain death burdens me; my situation differs in no wise from that of a man condemned to death and imprisoned in a room whose walls keep closing in upon him.
>
> Henceforth, there is nothing in my present existence that could not be destroyed (Sartre would say *néantiser*), and that precisely because my death is pressing in upon me. How could I escape being overcome by dizziness and succumbing to the temptation to make an end of this waiting, this miserable and uncertain respite, and thereby freeing myself from the torture of an immediate threat of death.

At that time I added: "*Therefore*, there arises for me a meta-problematic of no-longer-being, which is at once a doctrine of despair and a situation that can be removed only in suicide."

Some years ago I attempted to make this intelligible to the members of the Philosophical Society at Oxford, but in vain. It is noteworthy and also quite telling that they saw fit to condemn my attitude as reprehensible and shameful; they completely overlooked the fact that I was by no means rendering a value judgment; I was only enunciating the possibility that my situation could conceivably involve radical and inescapable despair.

It is the situation of any and every mortal being. And I think it is particularly important that we realize this when we come face to face with certain kinds of psychosis.

But what I would like to point out here is that this abyss which seems to be worrying me is in a certain sense a product of my freedom itself. Indeed, my death is nothing of itself or in itself (*in sich oder an sich*). It can claim the power of annihilation that it appears to possess only on the basis of a connivance with a freedom that actually betrays itself in providing such power. Only this type of freedom possesses the power to block the inexhaustible riches of the universe from my view. Therefore, my freedom has become a concealing power. Clearly, then, if we may speak of an ontological counterpoise to death, it cannot be life itself, since it actually tends so strongly to unite itself with what destroys it; nor can it be an objective truth of whatever sort. The ontological counterpoise can lie only in the positive use of freedom in rejecting the pernicious self-deception that induces life to transfer to death a power that it alone has a right to use. Freedom then acquires a new meaning: it becomes affirmation and love; and death is thus transcended.

In principle, I still believe what I wrote 22 years ago. Only, in the light of the fearful experiences that have since been my lot, I would now consider it proper to add the following observation: Unfortunately, it has been our fate to see before our very eyes how death-dealing machinery has been developed and perfected with the consequence that our range of freedom has been curtailed. This narrowing process is so far advanced that, for all practical purposes, we might conceivably speak of the abolition of freedom-space. Twelve years later I wrote in my book *Hommes contra l'humain*:

> Each of us who is not prepared to deceive himself or to become guilty of an assumption that is completely unjustifiable must admit that there are concrete means that could be employed against him and tomorrow divest him of a sovereignty, or even only a control, over himself, which at other times (think of the Stoics) would rightly be considered inalienable.

Along this same line, I would like to point out that a meditation such as I am conducting in your presence today also presupposes an area of security without which it would simply break down and cease.

The foregoing considerations show that it is impossible to conceive, with Heidegger in his *Being and Time*, the "being unto death" (*Sein zum Tode*) as a conditioning moment of my being. I would like to take up this problem as to its linguistic expression: being unto death. I have often called attention to the fact that the preposition "to"—if it expresses any relationship at all—expresses a relationship that is far from being clear. The clarity we are able to force out of it implies that I limit the statement to my body, indeed, to my body as a purely biological entity. But as soon as I think of myself as a unity, as an incarnate, present being, the ambiguity of the "to-relationship" appears in very glaring light. The French translator will have to point out this ambiguity. The expression *être pour la mort* intimates a *practical* purpose that is surely not intended in the expression *Sein zum Tode*. On the other hand, if he does not translate this *zu* (unto) with the word *für* (for), but instead with the word for turning toward something, *vers*, then he is not using correct French idiom. *Vers* presupposes a verb of motion. But the verb *être* (to be) cannot be used as such.

I, personally, feel that this is merely an external sign of something very profound. The lack of clarity in the language betrays a basic vagueness in the conception. Thus, one will or will not overhear in the word *zu* the severity of the inevitable condemnation as it is so admirably expressed by Brahms in his *Requiem*. If one does perceive the condemnation in *zu*, then the condemnation can unexpectedly empty itself of its ethical-religious meaning and one falls back into the world of law. In addition, one forsakes the existential order and reverts to contemplating a nature of which man is but one particular part. The question, however, still persists *whether* or not I actually desert nature in some measure as soon as I pronounce the "I."

Taken as a whole, the conclusions to be drawn from these considerations can only be expressed in the negative. If I proceed

from myself as subject, instead of dispassionately putting myself
on a par with my body considered as an object, then I *cannot* unequivocally determine my relationship toward my own death.
This relationship is a matter of choice; it has to be created; in a
certain sense it must be discovered.

However, we ought not forget that there is a profound reason
for the situation; namely, because the relation between the "I"
and what I call my body cannot be determined unequivocally.
It is my business to investigate the relationship personally. I can,
for example, regard my body in such a fashion that my life and
my being become crassly materialistic. On the other hand, men
like Bergson and Arnold Reymond have demonstrated in a sense
the proof of the invincibility of their spirituality by the manner in which they stood the physical test allotted to them.

It is now time to show that what I just said about my attitude
toward my own death becomes still more intelligible when I
consider my attitude toward the death of others. And here I
would like to be as concrete as possible.

To be among others evidently belongs to what I am, without
distinguishing now whether essentially or existentially, or even
without considering whether this distinction is applicable here at
all. But I will admit that I am fully aware that, as soon as I examine it in the concrete, this apparently simple statement "to
be among others" conceals a very complex reality which cannot
be absorbed in the fact that one unity exists among other unities.

Two elements in the expression "to be among others" can conceivably shift their meaning. The two components are *being
among*, and *the others*, the fact of being different. Certain people
go to make up my environment (my family, my profession, and
so on), and this environment in turn constantly supports me, and
without it I would be literally lost. Other people—to go a step
further—keep up what I might call "everyday" relations with me
(sales clerks, a bus driver, and so on) ; and, finally, there are those
who comprise the far greater number who are only passers-by,
people whom I meet occasionally and who, as far as I am concerned, might just as well be non-existent. In this last case, the
word "among" has no existential significance. So you see, the

word "the other," or "the others," in the phrase "being among others" does not always have the same meaning.

Now, this will give you some idea how I understand the word "survive." This word has genuine significance only when I am speaking about my relatives or about people who stand in much the same relation to me as my teacher, my pupils, or those with whom I am actually working to produce something. But obviously the basic problem, if we can even speak of a problem, arises particularly with regard to those I am bound to by ties of friendship, familiarity or love to such a degree that their disappearance would inflict a serious wound upon my person. I can say quite frankly that this is one of the fundamental questions I have pondered for half a century. You see, I have had to understand (and I publicly mentioned it in 1937 to the International Philosophy Convention) that on account of the abyss that was caused by the disappearance of someone I loved dearly, I experienced a wholly different and probably more profound pain than I actually suffer in the face of my own "having to die." It is quite possible that I can be numb to my own death, particularly if I am withdrawing from the world or see the world withdrawing from me. Genuine sadness, however, excludes insensibility; in fact, it would look upon any such narcosis as a betrayal.

There is of course an obvious objection. It could be said that we are dealing with purely subjective moods, with psychological impulses, that in no way change what we would probably call reality. But just what is this reality people generally like to talk about? If it is not outright fate, it is at least a controllable process by which the body—whether of a loved one or anyone else—becomes a cadaver and eventually disintegrates. However, limiting the reality of death to this biological process, whether consciously or not, means capitulating to the grossest materialism. That is so obvious I am almost ashamed to call it to your attention. When we speak of the dead in the present tense—of Molière, Mozart or Rembrandt, for example—we are obviously not thinking of their bodies that have long since decayed. Of course one might shrug his shoulders and scornfully remind me that what still remains of these men, or what we might speak of in the present tense, is their *work*, and their work certainly still

exists in material form. True as this may be, a response of this
sort is extremely superficial, for what perdures in material form,
and what will continue to perdure, are spirit and thought. If it
is to have any personal appeal, it will have to be adequately related to our spirit and our thinking. History shows that events
can intervene which actually make a certain language no longer
intelligible. But over and above this possibility, I will admit that
the word "outlive" is highly ambiguous. If it is true, from the
standpoint of time, then it is true in an infinitely more profound sense that they are the ones who actually outlive us. Here,
the prefix "out" means about the same as "over" in the phrase
"fly over." Molière and Mozart outlive us and illuminate us from
above.

To a certain extent everyone, or nearly everyone, will acknowledge this fact; but people generally do not want to admit it has
any metaphysical meaning. Just when we want an exact statement
as to what "spirit" really is, people generally remain vague to
the point of impoliteness; or perhaps they might even consider
it important to point out that the spirit in question is not the individual Mozart or Molière, whatever their fate after death may
have been.

Now, to return, mourning is not vague by any means. Where
it is kept alive from within by love, it seems to be accompanied by
the protestation in the second person: "You cannot simply have
disappeared; if I believed that I would be a traitor."

Naturally, there are certain types of philosophy that would
glibly dispose of this protestation as wishful thinking on our part.
That is particularly true of every species of Spinozistic philosophy; our statement would simply be dismissed as an illusion
based on a misunderstanding of the natural order of things. This
man whose utter disappearance or, better, whose annihilation
I find unthinkable, would, in this view, simply have been a very
fragile structure that eventually fell apart.

But here the distinction between what is objective and what
is existential is of utmost importance. There is no sense in saying
that the creature I loved was a structure, for this designation applies only to things. Love can only devote itself to a subject, that
is, to a being that is able to give love in return. Outside the spe-

cific dimension I call "intersubjectivity," there is no love deserving of the name; and the question about which our discussion revolves must and can be approached from this dimension alone.

If we speak of "being unto death" or "being headed for death," like Heidegger does, we are actually defending a species of existential solipsism, whether we are aware of it or not. For we are discussing the death of someone else as if we were witnessing it as an event, whereas in fact it does not touch me at all in the active sense of the word, even though I certainly may be interested in it.

Valentine, one of the characters in my *l'Horizon*, says of the man she loved and who has died in an accident: "His death is my death." Her protestation is sparked by absolute pain. Here is an instance of the tragedy of surviving. Crushed by death, the creature nonetheless seems to live on; it bears this contradiction within itself; no, it *is* this contradiction. Anyone who has ever experienced this situation can testify existentially to the falsehood of Spinoza's statement; his painful testimony is voiced in the dimension of intersubjectivity, something Spinoza knew nothing about. A long time ago, I felt obliged to point out that in a famous sentence of his *Ethics* Spinoza actually confuses the concepts of wish and hope, and, therefore, he fails to recognize the latter's specific character that justifies our considering it as a theological virtue. How could one do that with a mere "wish"?

But I believe there is still one other source of confusion that has proved to be equally disastrous, namely, that of Kant, who treats immortality as a postulate of the practical reason. In his anxious desire to exclude all feeling and sentiment, Kant appears to have misunderstood radically a fact that Plato, perhaps, but certainly Augustine and his entire school, brought into the limelight; namely, that love. Insofar as it is love, it exhibits an incomparable dignity by which it transcends mere feeling. However, in passing, I think I should call your attention to the ambiguity of the word "feeling"—one of the ambiguities that have introduced so much confusion into psychology.

What the mystics, rather than philosophers, have recognized is this: love and hope must not be separated. For a person without love, hope is not possible, only lust and ambition; and every ambition seeks to acquire some satisfaction for itself. But what good will such things be after death?

Even if it is not perfectly evident that death puts everything into its proper perspective, at least it irons out the wrinkles. Yes, wrinkles; is this not the image that comes to mind when we think of the purely ephemeral successes of anyone who has acquired property, power or publicity? Hope, on the other hand, looks far out above this wrinkled world of ours, and precisely therein lies the secret, or even the proof, of its transcendence. And the fact that it can strike root in us is the pledge, as it were, of what it proclaims. Just as concupiscence belongs to the world, so hope belongs to heaven, the only place where it will find its fulfillment.

What do I mean? Someone might object that the notion of "heaven" is meaningless anyway; are we supposed to imagine, he may ask, that what takes place in death and through death is a migration to another planet or another solar system? And supposing we reject this rather mythical conception, what else can the word "heaven" signify?

This might be one way to answer: Whatever speculative errors idealism may have been guilty of, it has at least earned the immeasurable credit of having made accessible to human understanding a fundamental truth that the Christian religion has been teaching from the beginning, namely, that there is a sense in which the soul goes beyond the visible world and in which the visible world becomes interior to it. What can that mean but that the visible world, the heavens of the astronomers with its billions of constellations, can itself become a symbol. The act of transcending, probably the highest act of which the human mind is capable, might well consist of precisely this conversion, where the visible becomes the actual symbol of a particular spiritual reality, and hence appears to be suspended from it. At this point I will refrain from taking up a declaration that transpires at the very core of mysticism and perhaps also at the heart of every theology worthy of the name. All I would like to do is remind you that even someone who has not directly participated in a mystical experience is able to travel the same path with only his own personal experience, provided, of course, that his experience is profound enough.

Perhaps at this point in our meditation we ought to recall briefly the most important points we have covered so far.

In the first place, it is not true at all that I have to think of myself as *destined for death*. There is no such *unequivocal* relationship that can be known by everyone. If there is such an unequivocal relationship at all, then it is only for the body as an object, that is, insofar as I isolate it from its mysterious ties with the subject, namely, myself. I repeat, there is no relation between myself as subject and my body that could be defined in an unequivocal and generally valid manner. I have to establish my own relationships with my body; I have to originate and even invent them. Here the experience of sickness is of outstanding value. We know beyond a shadow of a doubt that a person who falls victim to a disease can change and sublimate what at first looks like a purely biological exigency. Therefore, death—my death (and I understand this to mean the death of a human being)—begins to appear as something mysterious, and we would be guilty of a paralogism were we to confuse death with the unavoidable process that takes place within the body. I said "unavoidable" on the basis of what seems to be apparent enough to permit such a statement. But certain signs—which each of us ought to perceive with reverent attention—could very well create in us the presumption that mercy, which infinitely exceeds the limits of our reason, can, as it were, trickle through the mesh of determinism.

I then went over rather abruptly to the problem (if it really is a problem) that the death of a loved one poses for me. In contrast to what almost all philosophers have apparently thought, I maintain that this problem is more fundamental than that of my own death. Admittedly, I cannot thoroughly dismiss the problem of my own death, but I certainly can suppress it; I can become morally lazy in this regard. I can accustom myself to thinking of my own death as the beginning of a long-earned rest after the grueling work of a lifetime. But the death of someone else—one who was virtually another self to me—immediately shocks me into awareness. A bond has been broken, and I can hardly bear it. And yet it is not really broken, for even after the separation I am even more intimately united with the person who is no longer at my side than before. This contradiction is precisely the unbearable element. It involves a scandal that casts a disgraceful shadow of absurdity over the reality.

But here, too, and even more profoundly than before, freedom can enter into the situation—the only real and positive freedom, the freedom that is identical with love. Certainly, love forms an arch that reaches from selfishness to surrender (a distinction I have borrowed from Dr. Stocker and his neo-Augustinian vision). At this point I would like to define the deeper meaning of such surrender. If I had the time, I would select an example from one of my own plays, nearly all of which center around the themes I have been calling to your attention.

There is Aline Fortier in *Chapelle Ardente* (*The Funeral Pyre*), the woman who remains chained, as it were, to her dead son and in her fantasy exchanges places with him, though not without betraying him in the process. She makes a strenuous effort to dissuade her son's widow from any new love and presses her to marry a sick man whom the dead man could not possibly envy. She represents an extreme example of a possessive love that tries to hold fast to its object even beyond death.

Werner Schnee in *Le Dard*, on the contrary, is true to his friend until the end, a Jewish pianist who falls victim to the Nazi police, and rises to complete resignation. The same is true of Simon Bernauer in *Signe de la Croix*.

At this point someone might ask: What guarantee do we have that all this does not take place in the consciousness of the survivors, and that Aline's son and Werner's friend are ultimately nothing more than high ideals projected by the mourners? This prompts us to question a distinction that people not only generally accept but even imprudently endow with an absolute value it hardly possesses. It is a matter of distinguishing what is within us from what is outside us.

I naturally consider this distinction essential in determining our activity on the level of daily experience and even on the level of engaging other persons. It is part of the price we have to pay for the incarnation. I take a very good friend to the railway station; I take leave of him, and, now that he is gone, I ask myself where he is and what he is doing. I have at my disposal certain empirical means of getting in touch with him; he can send news to me, and I can send news to him. But this does not mean—and this is important—that under certain exceptional conditions over which I have no control, we could not meet in some other manner than those suggested. I hardly think we can honestly question the reality of *telepathy* anymore. And while I would be the first to admit that we usually act as though there were no such thing as telepathy and generally obtain all the information we need by letters, telegrams, telephone or radio, I think it is obvious that this visible world of ours, where I move about within a system of coordinates, is not the whole world; in fact, it may be only the most superficial portion of what is real. We only have to consider such generally inadequate notions as "unconscious" and "subconscious" to realize that in the areas to which these words refer it is no longer possible to draw boundaries between his world and my world. "You yourself? I myself?" Claire asks in *Quatuor en Fa dièze.* "Where does a personality begin?" The answer is forthcoming as soon as we enter the region where, under conditions about which we know practically nothing, the encounter between the living and those to whom we apply the insulting and desecrating expression "dead" takes place.

"The shallow, despised brook-death," says Mallarmé. Here again we find, though on an infinitely more familiar level, what I said earlier about Molière and Mozart: We are outlived by the very people we think we are outliving.

"That still remains to be proved," you might say. But let us note well under what conditions a verification is possible. Long ago, in my first *Metaphysical Journal,* I believe I proposed that every verification presupposes a triadic relationship, or, for that matter, the possibility that a "You" can become a "He." But as long as love is free from all possessive desire, it appears to be on the level of the dyad, that is, on the level where a "You" can *never* be converted into a "He." What we were discussing just a moment ago transpires precisely on this level; it is here that someone who has passed away can inhabit, so to speak, the living. To perhaps corroborate our findings one might point to the opposite role which suspicion, mistrust and the lack of discipline play in the works of Proust, especially in *Albertine disparue*

where we find the characters vehemently involved with a possessive desire for what ultimately remains denied them. Our
point is that the more we rise to generous love, the more closely
we approach a dyadic level where all control is superseded and
becomes superfluous. But I am not about to oversimplify the
matter. If a deceased person makes his identity known to me by
some visible sign, I will expect some kind of verification. But
where contact occurs without any external indications of what
is going on, where the presence of the deceased habitually haunts
the survivor, so to speak, and that so strongly that it becomes almost unimportant to know whether *I* speak or whether *he* speaks
since we are now a single entity—here the thought of verification
wilts and falls like a yellow leaf.

Now you know why I was resolved not to make any thoughts
about the beyond and what happens there, much less to describe
it. Not that such a description is impossible. I simply cannot
share the perspective that would allow such a description. I am
convinced that in the bosom of this strange life of ours, we exist
in such a way that the beyond has to remain *beyond*. Paradoxical
as it may seem, only on this condition can the beyond become
present, but as a mystery that we can only begin to fathom without the aid of theology. In the almost total night surrounding
us with a density that at times threatens to suffocate us, I believe
there is nevertheless an occasional illumination—signs, as it
were, that confirm our expectation and satisfy the personal demand which constitutes our very being.

But experience goes to show that this demand can be quite
deceptive, and for one who harbors it deep within himself it can
become so effaced as to be beyond recognition. The curse which
is inherent in the world and which is trying to take shape on
our every side consists in the fact that the world is constantly
trying to make our demand look absurd, antiquated and even
childish, and, unfortunately, the world finds an only too willing
accomplice in whatever tends to provoke despair. If my work as
a whole has any meaning at all, it is to demonstrate that there
can be a philosophy that helps uncover this demand (since for
the far greater part it is hidden) and, most importantly, serves to
strengthen and encourage it. It teaches men all over again how

to breathe; it wakes them up as a mother awakens her child when the moment comes to give him life. To awaken, to nourish, to teach men to breathe: these basic functions are reflected in the only philosophy I consider to be of any value; it can help us live, and (who knows?) to prepare ourselves along the paths of *docta ignorantia* for the ineffable amazement that awaits us on the eternal morning.

I am aware that this meditation can hardly be considered a lecture in the classical sense. However, perhaps a few words will make my meaning clear. Ever since I embraced the Catholic faith, I have very often said that I regard myself as a philosopher of the threshold, and I have always tried to act accordingly. I am perhaps even more sympathetic to those who are still groping and anxiously seeking, than to those who have been granted an infallible faith and, consequently, no longer need me. Our un-baptized fellowmen, of whom Claudel has spoken so well, are leading a shallow life. It is in the role of a philosopher of the threshold that I wanted to speak today. I have tried to see things as a prisoner would, and have tried to make a few cracks in our place of confinement. These fissures are bound to get larger due to the irresistible pressure being applied from the other side, and sooner or later the light of revelation will eventually stream in. But unfortunately there are priests who are too deeply absorbed in the social side of Christianity, priests slightly infected with Marxist dogmatism who are running the risk of losing sight of what I should like to call the "light of the beyond." The best answer they can give to the fearful questions of the afflicted is a hollow platitude. Not long ago I was told about a Dominican who frankly admitted he could not believe in immortality. Did he believe in the resurrection of the flesh? If not, what kind of sophistry did he have to use to quiet his conscience when he prayed the Credo at Mass each morning?

I would like to believe he is an exception. But I am afraid that many self-proclaimed Christians overlook an extremely dan-gerous form of secularization. What Berdyaev said about Com-munism can also be applied to spiritism: it actually developed because of the severe lack of genuine Christian thinking.

Theological reflection—and this I say not as a philosopher of the threshold but as a Catholic—should concentrate on the central questions I have raised today, not only because they provide interesting matter for speculation, but because of the unspeakable misery of innumerable, helpless souls who are in danger of being sucked into the propeller of a merciless world. Even the promise of a trip to the stars does not make this horrible prospect one iota more agreeable.

V

Martin Buber's
Philosophical Anthropology

It was with some reluctance that I accepted the invitation of my friend Pastor Ruf to come here again and speak to you about the philosophical thought of Martin Buber. But in view of the undeniable similarity between his and my own philosophical efforts, I finally came to the conclusion that it would not be right for me to decline.

It is not my intention here to go into the details of Martin Buber's personal history. I will limit myself to reminding you that he was born in Vienna in 1878, the son of a well-to-do middle-class family. As the result of an altercation between his parents, his mother left the house, and Buber did not see her again until his adult years. But from precious hints he has left us we learn that his boyhood and youth were happy just the same. He spent his early life first in the home of his grandparents and, later on, in Vienna where he familiarized himself with the masterworks of the arts and literature. As far as I can see there is nothing to indicate that the young Martin Buber, living as he did in a world poisoned with anti-Semitism, ever suffered from the fact that he was a Jew.

What spontaneously comes to mind when one tries to characterize this personality and his life is the word "fullness." There is a richness that captivates at first sight and is full of endless surprises. I had this feeling of fullness in my first and only encounter with Buber about ten years ago in a Paris hotel. And the other impression, closely associated to the first, was that of dignity. I had the feeling during this unforgettable hour as though one of the most sublime figures of the Old Testament had suddenly materialized before me.

Buber has labeled himself an atypical man. He was well aware that he was unclassifiable. And this brings him, if I may take the liberty of saying so, rather close to myself, for I, too, have again and again been faced with the fact that I am very difficult to classify. In his own mind Buber was neither exclusively a philosopher nor a theologian. Nevertheless, I see nothing wrong in dealing with his work solely under its philosophical aspect.

I want to choose as a motto for this lecture the following lines from one of Buber's later publications:

> Since I matured to a life lived on the basis of my own experience (a process which began shortly before World War I and ended soon after it) I have felt obliged to contribute the sum of my decisive experiences to the treasury of human thought, yet not so much as "my" experiences, but rather as valid and important insights for other people as well. Since I did not receive a specific message to transmit, but simply experienced certain things and gained a measure of insight, my communication had to be a philosophical one; that is, I had to transpose what had been a unique and singular experience into something everyone would be able to find in his own existence; I had to put what was essentially non-conceptual into concepts that could be (if sometimes only with difficulty) handled and communicated. More concretely, I had to turn what I had experienced in the I-Thou and as an I-Thou into an "It."

This is a key admission, and it throws into relief a number of features characteristic of Buber's thought. It shows that his thinking is based entirely on experience; it is essentially reflection on experience. At the same time it is open to anyone who can make use of it. I would even go so far as to say his thinking is in a profound sense *charismatic*.

In general we can say that Buber's thought began when it actually became fully aware of itself, that is, sometime between 1911 and 1919, and since then it has grown constantly and steadily like a tree.

There is no doubt that sometime around 1900 Buber was deeply influenced by the German mystics—from Eckhart to Angelius Silesius—and later on by the cabala; but subsequently he moved away from both these influences. However, we have reason to assume that he sensed or anticipated at a very early date—that is, even prior to 1900—the direction his thinking would eventually take. To document this we have only to look at his first philosophical publication, the important dialogue entitled *Daniel* which was published in 1913 by Inselverlag. I will do no more here than quote some particularly pregnant sentences from it in the hope they will introduce my own remarks a little further on:

> Whoever *truly* experiences the world, experiences it as a duality. He does not contemplate the world either with the close look of the woman who invests a great deal of care in the many details of a narrow foreground, nor with the far-reaching look of man for whom individual things are lost in the sweeping wave of a broad dynamism; he sees them with the eye of a human being; that is, he comprehends and discriminates, discerning in the playful stream of variety an essential line of tension; and to cope with this tension is precisely his task.

Even in this early work the philosophical as well as the poetic genius of Buber comes through. He already sheds light on the tension that exists between the "I" and the world, and he emphasizes the fact that the "I" is unthinkable without it. I want to stress the term "tension" at this early stage of our discussion because I, personally, find it preferable to the term "relation," which, as we are going to see, also plays an important part in Buber's philosophy. My particular concern at the moment is what Buber himself calls his philosophical anthropology.

Like Bernhard Groethuysen, who attended Dilthey's classes with Buber at the University of Berlin in the early 1900's, Buber is occupied primarily with the one, central question: What is

man? And he tries to formulate criteria that are typical of being
human. In his book *Das Problem des Menschen* (The Problem
of Man), which in my judgment is one of his finest writings, he
gives an historical presentation of the question, something which
philosophers as a rule avoid or only achieve at the expense of
making reductions that obfuscate the total view of the problem.

Buber sets out by making a crucial distinction:

> In the history of the human mind I distinguish epochs of
> the "safe home" and epochs of "homelessness." During the
> first, man lives in the world as in a house; otherwise, he
> lives in the world like on an open field. During the first
> epochs, anthropological thought is part of cosmology, but
> when man is "homeless," anthropological thought gains
> depth and independence.

Aristotelianism typifies the integration of anthropology into
cosmology. And Buber correctly observes the predominance of
the optical view in such philosophy, as in Greek thinking in general.

The world of Aristotle, however, was fated to collapse, and
primarily because Iranian as well as Christian thinking had become incapable of recognizing any truth outside the dualism
where man himself is the arena where the powers of darkness vie
with those of light. A new line of questioning was advanced in
its stead, primarily by St. Augustine. Asking with the Psalmist:
"What is man that thou art mindful of him?", the Augustinian
man is amazed at that in man which cannot be grasped as a part
of the world, or as one thing among others. In medieval thinking
man builds himself a new safe home, this time on a foundation
of faith, rather than on that of cosmology as the ancients had.

This new home, too, was eventually rocked to its very founda-
tions. We have to mention Pascal here, first of all, because no
thinker has seen as clearly as he did the unique character man
has on account of his position in the universe.

> Man is only a reed; he might even be the most fragile
> reed in nature—but he is a reed that thinks. It does not take
> the whole universe to come up against him to smash man;
> a haze, a drop of water will do to kill him. But even if the

universe were to destroy man he would still be more noble than what destroys him, because he knows that he dies, and he is aware of the universe overpowering him. The universe itself knows nothing about this.

So the paradox emerges: man knows himself as a part of the world and at the same time as a being that faces it.

Spinoza then makes the grandiose attempt to restore the lost unity. The reconciliation can be achieved, however, only in the minds of a few wise men, and this is sufficient to characterize his solution as a purely abstract one. A jarring note remains, even in Goethe, and even where he, under the guise of agreement, pushes beyond Spinozism.

In his reply to Pascal, Kant gives the impression he is actually resolving the antinomy:

That which comes up from the world to confront and startle you, the mystery of the world's space and its time, is the mystery of your own comprehension of the world and of your own nature. Your question therefore: "What is man?" is a genuine question to which you must seek the answer.

Anthropology, however, did not have a complete answer to this question.

The Hegelian panlogism claims to be able to give man a new definition of himself when it declares that reason is the true basic ground of the world, and the world is nothing but reason evolved and/or realized in the dialectical process; that the order in history is merely the realization of the Absolute Mind. But whatever triumph there was, was short-lived. Pascal's anxiety is not completely eliminated or allayed, and most probably because "a philosophical view of the world built on time can never quite convey that same feeling of safety that one built on space can." What had been lost, Buber profoundly remarks, was an element of confidence that a philosophy of "becoming" is evidently unable to preserve.

Buber by no means denies the historical importance of Marx's sociological reduction. Buber points out that Marx's principal error was not to take into consideration the fact that decision in man has the character of the irreducible. In Buber's opinion, among the pupils of Hegel, Feuerbach made a far more decisive contribution to philosophical anthropology than Marx. This is evidenced by the following passage quoted from Feuerbach:

> The individual man does not have the essence of man in himself, neither as a moral nor as a thinking being. The essence of man is only in the human community, in the unity of man with man; a unity, however, which is based on the reality of the distinction between "I" and "Thou."

A significant formula. Buber says it was a revelation to him even in his youth. Always ready to acknowledge his debts, Buber points out that, already half a century before Feuerbach, Jacobi and Humboldt discovered the value of the relationship between the "I" and the "Thou."

Nietzsche, who owes more to Feuerbach than is usually admitted, has the distinction of having been the first to raise the anthropological question in its full scope. Nietzsche realizes that man is essentially a problem unto himself. However, the solution he offers is unacceptable because the Nietzschean concept of the "will to power" is extremely dubious. It leads to a distorted and thoroughly dangerous notion of human greatness that ignores the responsibility which the truly great person bears.

Buber himself then tries to define the characteristics of the contemporary crisis. First of all he points to the disintegration of the old, organic forms of communal life such as the family, the estates, the guilds. The newer forms that have arisen in our time, such as the trade unions, for example, appear unable to revive the forfeited feeling of confidence and assurance. Another factor is that man is literally dominated by the products of his own labors. This is true primarily in the field of technology where man is about to be manipulated by the very machines he has invented. But it is even more true in the political sphere where, as we have seen, demons were generated that were beyond man's control.

Husserl, in his book on the crisis of European science in 1936, took great pains to demonstrate how necessary it is that man become fully conscious of his own predicament. And he was right in saying that "humanity in general essentially means being human in generatively and socially connected humanities."

At this point we should point out that naturally enough Buber thought Kierkegaard was the pioneer of true philosophical anthropology; he prepared the soil, so to speak, in which Feuerbach was to cultivate his fertile intuition. Unfortunately this never came about, since Feuerbach himself failed to come up with all the conclusions.

Decisive is the emergence of the category of the individual in Kierkegaard's thinking.

Particularly in his book *Die Frage an den Einzelnen* (*The Question Asked of the Individual*) Buber elaborated at great length the relationship between the individual and God as Kierkegaard saw it: to become an individual means to put oneself into an exclusive relationship with God—a relationship which makes all other relationships inconsequential. Buber, incidentally, takes Kierkegaard to task for apparently having forgotten that the relationship to the absolute "Thou" cannot be exclusive; on the contrary, it must be inclusive, so that the Danish philosopher's renunciation of Regine might have been the result of an error.

It would probably be worthwhile to study in detail Buber's criticism of Heidegger's philosophy. Buber regards Heidegger as a secularizer whose philosophy is doomed to failure because it evolves outside of a true concept of intersubjectivity. In the final analysis it is because Heidegger has never known the true "Thou" or the true "We."

> The person who is the mere object of my care is not a "Thou," but a "He" or a "She." The nameless, faceless crowd which swallows me up is not a "We," but a "One." But as there is a "Thou," so there is a genuine "We." This is a vital category for our analysis and we have to clarify it. With "We" I mean a group of several, independent persons, each grown up to his own self and his self-responsibility. The unity of the group rests on the foundation of this selfhood and self-responsibility and becomes possible through it. The specific character of the "We" is marked by the fact that there exists, or temporarily develops, a vital relation between its members. This means that in the "We" that

same ontic immediacy prevails which is the decisive prerequisite of the I-Thou relationship. The "We" potentially
includes the "Thou." Only persons who are capable of
truly relating to a "Thou" are able to form a true "We"
with one another. . . .

So we have to understand correctly that any group can only
be considered a true "We" if there is a real connection between
the individuals, and the individuals cooperate personally toward
a definite goal.

The essential "We" has up to now been much too little
recognized because it is rare, and because group formation
has hitherto mostly been considered as to its energies and
effects, but not as to its inner structure. Yet it is on the inner
structure that the direction of the energies and the quality
of the effects depend most strongly. . . .

We can summarize this brief historical survey by saying that
man helps us to truly know man only if he realizes the relations
possible to him with his whole being and throughout his life;
the question of what man is can ultimately be answered only by
the man who has arrived at solitude—a solitude, incidentally,
which itself has to be transcended if the person is to establish a
new and personal relationship with the world and with God.
"We might come closer to answering the question what man is
when we learn to understand man as the being in whom dialogical being-actually-two-together is realized in an encounter of two
persons."

Now, what distinguishes man from other living beings? Every
living being's habitat is its world. Buber feels, however, that the
word "world" is not suitable when applied to animals in its lit-
eral sense.

World necessarily means something that extends beyond
the area in which the viewer happens to be, and something
essentially independent of the viewer. . . . The area-image
of the animal is nothing but the dynamism of the sequence
of present moments connected to each other by physical
memory to the degree required by the vital functions to be
performed.

One could also, I would like to add, object to the use of the term "image" in this context. The term is not quite suited to a dynamic flux that is incapable of imagining itself. What is thoroughly original in the fact of humanity is the manner in which man confronts the world in all its independence. One has to add, though: "There is no 'existing-in-confrontation-with-a-world' which is not simultaneously a 'reacting-to-it-as-a-world,' and this implies that there exists an inchoative relationship."

Buber's most original contribution, however, is to have shown that varying and complementary categories come into play, depending on whether man faces things or his peers.

In the case of the I-It relation man dissociates himself from the thing he uses, reducing it, or augmenting it, to make it fit the function. But when man distinguishes another man from himself and thus gives him independent existence, he agrees to the fact that other beings, human like himself, live around him; and so man and only man is able to enter into relations with his peers and remain himself.

The very fact that we have language elucidates this. While the animal can call—and this is common to both man and animal—only man can address, and this implies a recognition of the other person as a subject. And that is the other person's realization. Here we are at the core of Buber's thinking. It is crucial to realize that for the person who observes or views another person, that other person remains an object, separate from himself, the subject. Things are totally different however "when in a receptive hour of my personal life I meet another person in whom something that I am unable to comprehend or enunciate conceptually 'tells me something'; that is, tells me, not what this person is or what is going on inside him or anything of this sort, but tells me something, means something to me, puts something into my life." This can signify that the other person needs me, for example. Or it can concern myself. In any event, it is a relation from subject to subject. Buber terms this kind of perception "becoming aware" (*Innewereden*). To "become aware" means "to perceive one's totality as spirit-determined personality, to perceive one's center which gives all one's utterances, actions and attitudes the distinct imprint of uniqueness."

It is obvious that perceiving the other person in this manner is basically different from the analytic and reductive cognition that is generally dealt with in epistemology. It would be wrong, by the way, to assume that Buber in any way neglects the vast area in which the I-It relation is effective. On the other hand, it is interesting to see that Buber hardly ever tends to interpret "becoming-aware" as intuition. At one point he even brings himself to criticize Bergson's notion of intuition. He prefers to speak of a real-phantasy, "a bold, flight-mighty, swinging empathy into the other's life, demanding my own being's most intensive stir."

Striking here is the poetic and highly suggestive quality of his formulation. Its grave disadvantage, to my mind, however, is that it can lead one to believe that "becoming aware" is a capability found only in a few especially talented people, whereas in reality this is a dynamic characteristic of humanity in general.

The term "attention" (Hinwendung) designates the "basic movement" which makes genuine dialogue possible. Analysis demonstrates, however, that there are certain factors working against the execution of this attending act, with the result that the dialogue all too frequently becomes spurious, as each participant remains a captive to his own subjectivity. Yet we must not overlook the fact that this subjectivity is initially not there, as idealism assumes it to be. On the contrary, subjectivity is a secondary phenomenon; it is the consequence of a treason of sorts that is perpetrated whenever a subject makes a false objectification, injecting into the area of the I-Thou the sort of relationship which is only applicable in the area of the I-It. I want to reemphasize, however, that Buber remains fully aware of the respective and complementary value of each area. He has made this abundantly clear on several occasions. It will suffice to quote the following text which was written toward the end of his life:

> By no means do I think that the life of the human mind, either in general or human thinking in particular, is exclusively made up of processes belonging to these two classes of relationship. What I mean is that whenever man takes a position toward the world or in general toward anything not

himself, or whenever he makes a basic statement, he actualizes either this "I" or that (the "I-You" or the "I-It").

But then he adds something very important:

> Authentic philosophizing ever freshly springs from a "fulguration" of the Thou-relationship which does not itself yield an objective perception or insight. Then the transposition is performed into the fixed order of the "It," and the end result might be, if the right workman was at work, the masonry of the system.

The term "fulguration" is not only adequate, it is also illuminating. Buber insists that I can become aware not only of another person, but also of an animal or a plant. Usually everyone is, as it were, armored against whatever it considers and deals with as an encroachment or an attack. There are moments, however, when the soul becomes receptive again, moments in which the concrete world assails me; it is simply that "creation which has been entrusted to me and everybody; in it we receive the signs of address." One cannot help sensing something of Berkley in this formulation.

Anyone who objects that Buber's treatment is overstepping the boundaries of anthropology would be ignoring the crucial fact that being human as such includes the antithesis of the other person, or, to get to the root of the problem, the antithesis of God. We are only about to overcome the crisis of our age if we do more than understand this intellectually; we will have to translate our understanding into actual living. One might wonder whether the objections Buber's thinking might evoke in some minds are not due to their being captives of an objectivistic conception of God.

I feel it appropriate again to refer to the statements that Buber himself has made in the above-mentioned work:

> I have once stated that speaking of God as "He" is a metaphor; speaking to God as "Thou" is not. . . . I want to make clear what I mean by this. Anyone speaking *of* God makes God into a being among other beings, into something that "is there," into a being with particular

characteristics. To speak *to* God, however, means nothing less than to turn to God himself. How is this possible, since God cannot be found in one direction rather than in another? The answer is: Nothing is required but total attention (*Hinwendung*). This attention is nothing but just that; in no way does the attentive one limit the "Thou" of his attention to being such and such and nothing else. There are no more metaphors involved.

This calls for some explanation. For an opponent could, after all, object that such attention is merely an operation of the mind. What right do we have, the opponent could ask, to attribute ontological privileges to this merely mental operation? Buber feels that human experience in its totality—or let us say, preferably, in its originality—provides the answer. But what Buber terms "attention" could we not just as well call *overture* or *openness*? I am using the term here in the sense that Bergson gave it in his *Les deux sources de la morale et de la religion* (The Two Sources of Morality and Religion). Did Buber know this work? And if he did, what did he think of it?

The psychologizing criticism implies a postulate which Buber expressly rejects, the postulate, namely, to claim the primacy of the separate Ego, equipped with some kind of *inseitas*, or being-in-itself. We have already shown to everybody's satisfaction that Buber rejects such a conception as totally false.

I feel tempted to put forward a small objection against Buber concerning the term "relation"; to my mind this term is suffused with generality and, what is more, it implies a concept, that is to say, objectivated data. We can probably best understand what is involved and meant here if we recall an actual encounter that was experienced as such. And let us not forget how difficult it is to find adequate terminology in this area! For example, when Buber uses the word "vis-à-vis" he does not, it seems to me, point up sufficiently the difference between what he wishes to capture in the term and "opposition" in the true sense. Yet I have to admit it is quite difficult to make the necessary distinction between the elements of "opposition" and of "co-presence on the scene." But I feel that some of the texts we cited sufficiently show

how Buber manages to catch our attention and stir us to such a degree that we feel obliged to respond.

In this kind of philosophy the concept of response is as central as that of responsibility. There can only be authentic responsibility where there is a genuine response. But response to what? "Every given hour with its contents of world and destiny is a personal message to whoever is attentive; being attentive is all that is required to start reading the signs one receives."

We might already guess at this point that the machinery of our civilization intervenes to obstruct or even stop this constant flow of messages. Conscience, on the other hand, consciousness in the moral and ethical sense of the word, is receptivity to these messages. And on this point Buber obviously differs with Heidegger. For the author of *Sein und Zeit* (Being and Time) "existence is a monologue." The man of authentic existence in Heidegger's mind is not the man who truly lives with other people, but rather a man "who knows true life only in dealing *with himself*."

We must return once more to the vexing question: Who speaks to us? Buber's answer seems to be of decisive importance. We must not reply: God—"unless we say it from the perspective of that deciding hour of personal existence when we had to forget everything that was handed down to us, learned, self-devised, every bit of book knowledge, and were immersed into obscure night." Buber uses the following comparison: To anyone who really wants to absorb a poem, biographical data about the poet are of no use; the "I" that he faces is the subject, the "I" of this particular, singular poem. The situation is entirely different when we want to get an idea about a particular poet by reading a number of his poems.

I would personally go even further than Buber; I would ask whether the question "who" should not be eliminated entirely. For the question aims ultimately at an identification that is only possible in the objective world, or where it is possible to establish certain criteria. (I have the identification in mind which police commissars are after.) But in our case the question is not: Is it he? but rather and explicitly: Is it you? The act by which I declare: "Yes, this is you," is beyond the possibility of an identification, because identification refers to a specific thing among other things. And it is precisely this "among others" that is impossible because of the singularity of the "Thou."

This is probably what Buber means anyway when he emphasizes the necessity of "holding on to God," as he puts it. He explains clearly that what one has to hold on to is not an image of God, or a concept one has of God, but God as being. He uses another comparison: The earth depends on the sun as existing, and not as some concept that the earth might conceivably have of the sun.

Evidently what is meant here by the term "holding on to" is faith in its specific sense.

In the introduction to the important treatise *Zwei Glaubensweisen* (Two Kinds of Faith) Buber stresses the difference which exists in his opinion between thinking as a rational function of the mind and faith in the proper sense. Rational thinking constitutes only a part or a partial function of my being. But when I believe "my whole being, my being in its totality, enters into the process; in fact, the process only becomes possible by virtue of the fact that my relation of faith is a relation of my whole being. Personal totality in this sense, however, can only be accomplished if the entire function of thinking is also integrated into the totality without impairment and is permitted to operate as subordinate to and determined by it."

We want to make sure at this point that there is no question of replacing the term "totality" with the term "feeling." Feeling is no way the whole; at best it is an indication that the being of man "is about to unite into a totality." But I am not quite sure that I understand exactly what Buber means here by the phrase "is about." In the main, however, his thought is clear, and it would certainly be a grave mistake to classify it as irrational. Buber, for example, wants to point out that confidence in the strict sense does not rest on any motives. Motives rather offer themselves in retrospect to the justifying consciousness. This does not make Buber's thinking irrational. For him, reason, if merged with the spirit, infinitely surpasses analytical and calculating reasoning.

It seems to me this is the point where we have to refer to the chapter "Der Mensch und sein Gebild" (Man and His Imagery) in the *Beitrage zu einer philosophischen Anthropologie* (Contributions to a Philosophical Anthropology). In this chapter, which mainly deals with art but also more briefly and less directly discusses love and faith, our philosopher poses this question: How is it that mankind was not satisfied with simply sifting out of its confrontation with the great unknown a sensorily perceived world reduced to its own proper size and form? To answer this we must go back to the encounter-situation.

In the face of the unknown X man has at first to rely on his senses to present as something familiar what is totally alien. But then he reaches beyond what the senses give him; he expects more, he wants a deeper figurative vision, for the sake of the figuration in work. Man transcends the utilized for the sake of the envisaged. What does this mean?

When we know the answer to this, we will be able to assign an anthropological locus not only to art but also to the other forces that enable man to transcend the boundaries of the "natural" and thus to establish the typically human area of existence. I would like to point out, incidentally, that Buber's thinking comes amazingly close here to Heidegger's as it is expressed, for example, in the *Brief uber den Humanismus* (Letter on Humanism). These forces—art, love and faith—are the true powers of cognition. They are all "against the alienation of the world."

This is where we again come across the idea of the "safe home" that we met earlier. It is in this perspective that we have to view the essential role of language. "The mystery of the genesis of language and that of the genesis of humanness are one and the same." Here we are at the nodal point of Buber's philosophy. Of particular importance, I think, is the statement: "The locus of the spoken word is the Between."

This category of the Between is essential. It goes without saying that this must not be thought of as a spatial category. Here I would like to point to the close kinship of Buber's and my own philosophical search, and I want only to add that Buber, in contrast to myself, does not seem to have interested himself in parapsychological research, especially with regard to telepathy, although these phenomena cast significant light on this reality of a non-spatial Between.

So we have returned full circle to Buber's central problem: the problem of dialogical life. Buber has repeatedly dealt with this problem, first of all in his famous *Ich und Du* (I and Thou), of course, but also in a much less known little piece entitled *Das Soziale und das Zwischenmenschliche* (Social and Interhuman Relations), in which he elaborates and formulates with great clarity the basic difference between social and dialogical communication. We must realize first, he says, that there might very well be a group where no personal relationship takes place between its members.

> By no means does mere membership in a group involve an essential relation between one member and another. There have been groups in history, true, which comprised even highly intensive and intimate relations between pairs of its members and encouraged them for the better cohesiveness of the group—for example homoerotic relations among the Japanese Samurai and the Doric warriors. In general, however, the leaders of groups, particularly in the more recent past, are more inclined to suppress the element of personal relations in favor of the purely collective element.

We cannot put enough stress on the ambiguity of relations between people that Buber so ardently exposes. For example, he recalls a demonstration in which he took part to do a friend a favor. He remembers himself walking in line, marching by the side of people he did not know. There was nothing resembling that interhuman relation which can only exist from one person to another where there is dialogue.

These insights, if rather general, must be taken into account if we are to find ways and means to lead mankind out of its present universal crisis. The question is how to get people out of the false dilemma between an imaginary individualism and a collectivism that denies the human personality.

The error of individualism lies in its spurious interpretation of solitude in the bosom of which the person defines and creates himself as an authentic individual. This solitude, although necessary, must be a springboard; solitude must be overcome and there must be no question of getting to like it and treating it as an absolute, for that means ignoring the tension between the "I" and the "Thou" which we now know is the truly necessary prerequisite if the "I" is not to get lost in what is unauthentic. Collectivism is no less injurious to the unity or totality of human existence. And both individualism and collectivism are the realization or manifestation of the same condition, only seen in different phases.

> This condition is characterized by the confluence of cosmic and social homelessness, fear of the world and life itself into an existential constitution of loneliness such as never before existed. At one and the same time the human person because he is human feels excluded from nature like an abandoned child, and because he is a person isolated in the midst of the uproarious world of man.

Here we meet again what we have recognized to be the central theme of Buber's philosophy, but we are now in a position to sense all its implications. In his *Philosophische Anthropologie* (Philosophical Anthropology) Buber has made his point decidedly clear. Here is one more explanation of the nature of the *true "We"*:

> The "We" that I am talking about is not something collective; it is not a group, or an objectively demonstrable plurality. The "We" belongs to speaking in the first person plural, as the "I" belongs to speaking in the first person singular. The "We," no more than the "I," cannot be actually preserved in speaking in the third person. But the "We" does not have the relative constancy and continuity that the "I" has. As a potential, the "We" lies at the basis of all history of the mind and of action; it actualizes itself unexpectedly time and again, and as often it deactualizes itself unexpectedly and is gone. The "I" can actualize itself within a group, and that group will then be composed of a fiery core and a slaggy crust; or it can flare up outside of all collectivity and glow. In the air of debate the "We" cannot breathe, and no assemblage of so-called "like-minded" people is able to say "We" authentically in the middle of a debate; but it still happens, even today, that in a gathering of multiple tongues all of a sudden the genuine "We" is alive in their speech.

A little further on in his text Buber shows us that man, although he always has conceived his ideas as an "I," placing them in the firmament of the mind, has always introduced his ideas into existence as a "We," using that modality of existence which Buber calls the Between, or inter-existence.

This means, if I interpret correctly, that the transition to existence—which is nothing else but faith—is made in the dimension of the "We," and in this dimension alone. Outside of the "We" there might be room for an idea or a thought incapable of transposing itself into existence. But it is the authentic "We" which is effective. Buber speaks of a leavening of the human race with genuine We-hood. Man, he tells us, cannot stay in existence unless he learns to persevere as an authentic "We."

It should be very useful to give these views deep and detailed thought. I for one would like to raise the question of whether it is right to substantivate the "We" in this manner. The word "We-hood" is a little jarring to my ears, and I wonder whether this might not have a very profound reason, having to do with the fact that precisely in the "We" there is something that balks at becoming a noun.

Before I conclude, I want to make a few observations on Buber's interpretation of guilt and guilt feelings.

Our author takes, as we will see presently, a very strong position against the temptation to which so many psychoanalysts and sociologists succumb; the temptation is to dissolve guilt as such into nothingness and to analyze only in what way guilt is felt or accepted. Buber is concerned with exploring guilt insofar as it is more than merely a psychological reaction or a taboo still existing in the depths of the unconscious.

Let us take a man who has burdened his conscience by acting in a certain way under exactly determined circumstances, or he may, on the contrary, have defaulted by omission, or he was a party to what might appear to him a collective guilt. After years he is still haunted by a sense of guilt. He is aware of the minute details of the evil he has perpetrated and is unable to keep his mind off them.

That which keeps attacking him has nothing whatsoever to do with a parental or societal censure, and if he has no retribution to fear from the temporal powers and does not believe in a retribution in the hereafter, there is no threat of punishment to scare him. What comes into play here is the penetrating insight that we cannot return to the point of departure and that what is done is irreparable; that is, the real insight into the irreversibility of time spent, a fact which is most inescapable in the perspective of one's own death, the strongest of all human perspectives. From no point is time more felt as fall than from the point of the guilty man's view of himself. Tumbling downward in this fall, the guilty party is visited by the horrors of being identical with himself. I, he is given to understand, who have changed, am still the same.

Existential guilt, that is the guilt with which a person as such has burdened himself, cannot be handled by such categories of analysis as repression or making-conscious. The guilty party is fully aware of the action he regrets. To be sure, he frequently tries to push this aside, but what is being pushed away is not the fact as such but its existential depth. The order of the world of man has been violated, and the guilty one knows and recognizes this order fully. This idea of order is of fundamental significance and precludes any possibility of a merely subjective interpretation. This explains why Buber categorically opposes the escape device to which Aldous Huxley, for example, resorts when he recommends the use of mescaline.

I would only like to point here to a certain terminological inconsistency when our philosopher speaks of the "objective relationship which two people have with one another." The use of the word "objective" seems objectionable to me, as it involves the danger of our being led back to a way of thinking that could be termed "preexistential." There is danger of confusing objectivity with actuality, something that can very easily happen. The deep meaning, however, is beyond any doubt. Buber is always concerned with awakening us to the awareness of interhuman relationships. The principal merit of Buber is to have focused the limelight on the structural rather than the formal conditions that are vital for humanity; if these conditions are not heeded it might well be that mankind degenerates right before our very eyes.

I would have liked to show in more detail how Buber throughout his life and with admirable persistence has made every effort to concretize his thought and put it into flesh and blood. I want to give at least one example that I feel is extremely typical. I have in mind the attitude Buber took in the Palestine conflict, and which exposed him to attacks from various quarters. He spoke out resolutely against the nationalism that inflamed the two communities against each other. He would have wanted very much to bring about some sort of coexistence, a *convivencia* between the two nations which, with the religious differences remaining intact, would have led them to respect one another. Buber was able to look beyond the present conditions and the aroused passions, whereas neither of the two communities could. In this Buber was the leader on a path whose end is still obscured by night.

I am the first to admit that this lecture only outlines a very small sector of Buber's thought. It would give me satisfaction, however, if my inadequate observations were to stir in some of you the desire to get in direct contact with his work. There is no special jargon in Buber; on the contrary, his writings are distinguished by a clarity seldom found in contemporary writers. I hardly have to mention that it is Buber's constant preoccupation with the other person that sets his thinking apart. The *other person* is not primarily a threat, as he is for Sartre, but rather a brother whom I must try to understand and on whom I can lean and rely even if I feel I have to oppose him.

VI

My Dramatic Works as
Viewed by the Philosopher

In my opinion even the most superficial consideration of the relationship between an author and his work reveals the weakness, not to say the inadequacy, of our routinized habits of thought. This is the reason I prefer to speak in the first person, as I am about to examine my own work and try to determine precisely how it is related to what I call my "I." The obvious question is: How do I propose to get hold of my entire work? To a casual observer I am sure it looks like a veritable patchwork of assorted books and articles.

Now, I presume—with no genuine assurance, I may add— that someday everything I have ever written will be assembled in a few substantial volumes with the legend: *Gabriel Marcel: Collected Works.* Also assuming—and this is even more tenuous —that this is about to occur in my own lifetime, I will actually be able to take my entire work in hand and find my way about without inordinate difficulty—provided, of course, that the volumes have a properly arranged table of contents and an index of subject matter. But at present an appreciable number of my writings are still scattered here and there and are quite difficult to locate. Assuming all this, then, would I in fact be any closer to actually coming to grips with everything I have written? I hardly think so. I find it difficult enough just to set up the problem properly, since a number of its hypotheses are far from clear.

You might ask why all this hair-splitting. It would seem that the truth of the matter is simple enough; everything printed in the Marcel volumes is the product of my pen. Far be it from me to argue the point—although I might simply add that I did dictate some of the pieces to my secretary. Yet everything I have written down in book form was initially jotted down in notebooks or on loose sheets of paper, and the innumerable individual characters were indeed written by my own hand. Is this perhaps a clue? Am I in the final analysis my hand?

One might be inclined to say this is absurd; my hand serves my entire person and that is *me!* But I think the expression "entire person" is apt to cause some confusion; it represents a very clumsy attempt to define what I spontaneously, but inaccurately, designate as "I." The central difficulty is thrown into sharp relief when we consider that my work, insofar as it belongs to me, apparently should stand in such a relationship with me, with what I am, that I could assume full responsibility for it. And this is hardly the case at all. Even if I were to go to the trouble to reread everything I have ever written (the very idea of doing such a thing already fills me with extreme reluctance), I would doubtless have to take cognizance of the fact that my whole person is by no means uniformly embodied in what I roughly designate as "my" work.

Were I to undertake this rereading, furthermore, I would, I am sure, be overwhelmed to see how far the water has receded from the shore it once washed. I think this image adequately reflects a profound reality. Take the first part of my *Metaphysical Journal* as an excellent case in point. When I first wrote these pages a few months prior to the outbreak of World War I, they were undoubtedly authentic statements about reality; they impressed me as a way I should follow, or, to be more precise, they were apparently preparing me for something to come. But today they seem so confused that I can hardly bear to read them.

In order to understand this properly, you will have to realize abstract reasoning is apt to be a hindrance. We are talking about an adventure. I was searching for no place in particular and I did not really know whom I would meet or what I was about to discover. The very uncertainty of the situation drove me on and sustained me. I was like an explorer who sets out to trace a river to its original source. All I could say beforehand is that I was starting in a definite direction.

Now, I am sure, from rereading some unpublished memoranda and, of course, the *Journal* I just mentioned, that my initial philosophical searchings were goal-oriented, and they had a definite point of departure. But now I feel I have entirely disengaged myself from these earlier attempts, or—what amounts to the same thing—I no longer feel I have any connection with them. It is not that I did not have the proper intellectual tools at the time; as I look back, I am sure that I did. But now they simply appear rudimentary and totally inadequate. The fact of the matter is I have lost the living contact that should ordinarily exist between a workman and his tools.

Apparently this point is important, so I would like to pursue it somewhat further. A moment ago I said I had a definite point of departure. But it is only after I had already begun my search that I realized it was illusory to believe my personal concrete situation was not going to have any effect upon my philosophical search; I believed my starting point was not going to have any bearing on my conclusions. But it was not long before I met with evidence that directly contradicted my original method; I suddenly saw that the empirical data that guided my thinking might not, in fact could not, be conceived independently of my own thought. To put it another way: the substantial being I call my "I" cannot rightly be separated from empirical data, for these are simply the data of my own existential becoming! It would be wrong to assert categorically that empirical data exists separately from the self-determination of thinking. When I look at it now, the question is much more complicated than I once imagined it, and perhaps I was unfair in accusing Fichte's system of completely ignoring "facticity," as it has come to be called, that supposedly fashions me as a separate individual.

The experience of what I then called the non-contingence of empirical data eventually led me to reject all formalism and to fix my attention on the definite significance of concrete situations. This provided the foundation for a career in dramatic art as I have always understood it: the representation of persons engaged *in definite situations*, apart from which men could only be represented through tainted *abstractions*. Unknown to me at the time, I began to actualize my basic tendency to combine my philosophical investigations with my theatrical creations. It might be interesting to note—and somewhat paradoxical—that my own concrete situation at the time (as I shall describe it in a moment) was still appreciably distant from my philosophical efforts; my own situation did not yet shine through my dramas as perhaps it should have; it had no effect on my manner of characterization.

As painful as it might be, I must sketch briefly that very basic situation to which I have already so often alluded and from which my inquiry was to proceed in *two directions*. In providing the information I hope to contribute something at least approaching an answer to the question of the relationship between my work and myself.

It will come as no surprise if I say I will have to take my family background into account. And I will begin with an experience I would properly call "metaphysical," namely the death of my mother; I feel it was the most decisive experience of my childhood. I was only four years old at the time, and she was snatched from me within forty-eight hours. Her death made it necessary that I be reared by my mother's own mother and by my mother's sister, who eventually married my father two years later. At this early age I was already deeply affected not only by the death of the person nearest me in life, but also by the unfortunate confusion that came about as a result.

I suppose someone looking at the situation quite dispassionately would say I did not have to suffer want, for it was obvious I was being pampered by the entire family. But below the surface my mother's sudden absence left a scar of anxiety in me that I found absolutely unintelligible. The agnosticism of my immediate life left me inconsolable, and in the small circle I became the center of almost constant attention. In an unpublished piece entitled *Le Petit Garçon* I had the principal character say: "I suffered from the fact I felt myself all too important." I feel I was too much in the limelight; I needed a little shade if I was going to exist peacefully. But this is only one of the disadvantages I suffered as an only child. How often I was deeply disturbed that I never had a brother or sister! They certainly would have been equal partners in conversation; they would have provided just that shade I needed. Instead, I had to populate my loneliness with all sorts of imaginary beings. And these became the real milieu of my early life, the atmosphere that eventually gave birth to my dramatic characters.

Furthermore, the anxiety with which my aunt devoted herself to me and watched over my physical, mental and moral health, tended to make of me in every regard an unsure, confused and clumsy creature. I also could not fail to notice the serious incompatibility of my father and my aunt; it was plain to see they were two entirely different people. I had the feeling that they only married on account of me, and they shared no genuine happiness. This may not have been my fault personally, but what is worse it was due to the very fact I existed at all. Admittedly, I cannot verify this hypothesis, but I am nonetheless inclined to think that under the stress of unmerited guilt, I acquired a sense of tragedy I was never to lose.

In 1896 my father was appointed French ambassador to Sweden. I loved the Swedish scenery. It suited my disposition of precocious severity, which, strangely enough, did not preclude childish behavior and spirits at times so high they actually disconcerted my own family. The stay in Sweden was short; my father found the climate disagreeable, and he availed himself of an opportunity to become a member of the French Council of State. I still remember quite vividly how dismayed I was on hearing the news. *I hated Paris.* I was all too aware that I would have to go back to school, and I was afraid.

School was nothing but one incessant achievement contest, and I dreaded it. This only heightened my already unhealthy anxiety. My father and stepmother had been brilliant students themselves and I was sure they would attach excessive importance to my always being at the head of the class. I found extremely painful the prospect of being judged solely on the merits of my grades and term averages, and in the background lurked the anxious question: Would I prove myself worthy of the sacrifices and privations this would cause my family? To be sure, I never articulated the question in so many words; it simply hung in the air, so to speak, poisoning the atmosphere and contributing to my feeling in those terrible years that whatever knowledge was imparted to me was actually tainted, because it merely served the purpose of testing my accomplishments over against those of my classmates. Needless to say, this further increased my anxiety. The experience engendered in me an aversion to instruction in the higher schools that never entirely disappeared. *With one exception: philosophy class! There for the first time I felt at home.* And if now I did outsoar my comrades it was not because of long hours of slaving and cramming. For my work was now in accord with a genuinely spontaneous desire. Work was a joy.

As I look back, philosophy was an experimental field where I thought I might be able to take revenge for my earlier state of servitude. By "servitude," however, I only meant to express the difficult situation I found myself in, perhaps best characterized in my family's assorted varieties of agnosticism. Of all my relatives, only one, my uncle's wife, practiced any religion at all. She was a devout Jewess. And I distinctly remember the humorous impression her vestigial religious practices made on me. Otherwise, my entire family subscribed to the widely held view that the findings of science, and even the dictates of conscience, could not be reconciled with the antiquated views of faith. Almost unconsciously I felt a need to free myself from this sort of ideological captivity. And while I never had a spark of revolt in me, I was strongly drawn to my aunt; she embodied moral duty in all its rigor, and later her devotion almost reached a form of holiness.

My relationship with my father was quite tense. Even I as his son found him one of the most disconcerting persons I have ever known. Like most brilliant people he could not bring himself to swallow a sarcastic remark or an ironic comment. Furthermore, he criticized my upbringing. People were pampering me, he said, and I almost felt disloyal in agreeing with him, even though I indeed suffered enough from the very object of his indictment. Many years later I put the following words into the mouth of

Raymond Chaviere; in the scene he is confronting Isabelle, the young woman who had just married his divorced father; he recalls his deceased mother, and says:

> Between my mother and me there existed complete intimacy; it brought with it moments of wonderful happiness, but I also saw my mother suffer for her own fault. I hastened in such moments to accede to her wishes and to adjust myself to her dreams; nevertheless, I lived in constant fear of disappointing her. Sometimes I was angry when she took as normal something that had meant a great deal of sacrifice on my part. And then I was ashamed for having been angry, and the vain attempts to forget or to seek reconciliation when some accidental slip, a word, a gesture, made my anger apparent.

The more I think about it, it seems that my complicated childhood situation drove me in the direction of the religious. I purposely did not say to "religion," because at the time I still could not bring myself to join any particular sect. But on the other hand I was very suspicious of every kind of religious syncretism —what I like to call "religious Esperanto." I began pursuing the facts that religious thinking supplied, very prudently, and without applying myself to a study of primitive religions for fear I might slip into sociology (for which I had little sympathy).

Everything that had happened to me previously awakened my will to be free. And anyone who is interested can trace my steps to freedom in my *Metaphysical Journal*. Simultaneously I felt compelled to acquire a measure of intellectual clarity and in turn to give expression to it in my dramatic works. From my present vantage point, my theater pieces, to a much larger extent than my philosophical works, appear to relate directly to that unique opportunity, that original gift, whereby every human being is able to find his particular place in the world.

Now, I am sure you will agree, a conference like this is hardly the place to make a painstaking analysis of all thirty of my plays from this point of view. But because it is so crucial to an understanding of my thought, I think it is only fitting we should pause a moment and perhaps look at what I consider a representative piece of my theatrical work, namely, *Le Quatuor en Fa dièze*.

It was in this play that I first indicated the use of music. Now, as you probably know, music has always played an important part in my own personal life; in fact at one time I even considered devoting myself to it exclusively, and had I not been dissuaded by my piano teacher I probably would have gone on to be a composer. As far back as I can remember, music provided me with a pleasant escape—not to mention the fact that it brought me closer to my father, for while my aunt was hopelessly unmusical, my father took avidly to music and was himself an enthusiastic musician.

Le Quatuor en Fa dièze entails two peculiar elements: the one is quite apparent, the other not so. When I was a boy of ten, my family sustained a hard blow; my uncle got a divorce, and while he was doubtless at fault my grandmother, perhaps naturally, sided with her son. My father, on the other hand, was anything but sympathetic, and made no effort whatever to conceal his feelings from my uncle; he even continued to invite my divorced aunt to musical evenings he arranged, thereby vexing my grandmother no end.

With a few alterations, I incorporated this situation into my play. Roger Mazére manages to stay on good relations with his sister-in-law, Claire, even after his brother Stefane, a composer, has divorced her, and eventually he takes her as his own wife. For Roger this seems hardly a reason to sever relations with his own brother, and he keeps in touch with him in spite of Claire's unjustified insistence to the contrary.

Looking back now, I have to admit, indeed against my will, that the latent opposition between my relatives found expression in the conflict between Stefane and Claire. Claire embodied moral intransigence and sternness, especially in matters that had anything to do with sexual love; that was also the characteristic trait of my aunt. The composer generally resembled my father, especially with his esthetic dilettantism and his none too rigid view of conjugal relations. I might also say—and this is the first time it so clearly occurred to me—Roger in some way embodies me, for his was surely my situation: a son torn between two persons, one the embodiment of moral consciousness, and the other an artist who looked full face into the world with all its pomps. Just as Roger married Claire, I enthusiastically took my aunt's part. And just as Roger continued to visit his brother, I, too, refused to sever the secret bonds that, in spite of everything, bound me to a world I found lacking ethical conviction. Roger suffers because he is not creative. The only thing he feels capable of is sympathy almost to excess. And that is exactly how I felt up to a point, since I was so deeply involved in the situation I just described.

If I have spent so much time discussing this aspect of my early works, it was only because I wanted to demonstrate to what extent one has to look for the roots of this particular play in an existential situation rather than in the concept. Indeed, the concepts play a much more exaggerated role in my first two dramas, *La Grâce* and *Le Palais de Sable*; but from *Le Quatuor* and *L'Iconoclaste* onwards the actual source of my theater creations was existential bonds. This becomes even more apparent in the works I wrote after my marriage in 1919.

Now, with these lengthy and complicated explanations out of the way, I would like to return to my opening question: What is the relationship between me and my work? Without hoping to give an exhaustive answer, I think I can sagely say this: If I have a right to speak of a realization of my own ego in my works, it is only to the extent that this "I" has gradually discovered the underlying unity of itself that was initially disguised under separate aspects. This unity can only be understood dynamically. I would like to call its dynamism-element "impetus." The more we meditate on this unity, the more likely we are to see that it stems from a combination of creative activity itself and a philosophy of creative activity. This is what I have been so often emphasizing over the last ten years: In my works, drama, by and large, definitely takes precedence over philosophy. Still, this does not justify the conclusion that in general my own personal biographical references dominate my dramas. I would even say the contrary is true; such references become less and less evident. At first only a very general theme-field gradually takes shape, which then often develops in some way we least likely expect. Consequently, the great events of this tragic period of my history more and more distinctly assume their rightful perspectives.

I should like to discuss several themes that appear to be particularly illustrative.

In order to investigate this fund of themes even superficially, I had to depend on scattered, uncollated and unpublished notes, of which I have only a rather vague memory. However, not long ago, I was fortunate in finding a small notebook that helped me establish an interesting fact: In 1919 or 1920, I had sketched a theme that, with later alterations, took form in my play *Un homme de Dieu*; I also incorporated it in *La Chapelle Ardente* (The Funeral Pyre), although in their present form the two plays have nothing in common. In those days everything developed as if to provide me with my own personal "time of plenty," and I fashioned the basic elements that were later reflected in my characters. I kept each element strictly separated from each other and each had its own proper life story. Doubtless, a great many dramatists and novelists have the same experience.

What I think is the most crucial problem now is actually cultivating my allotted "land" of plenty. I spent so much time on this point earlier to show just how this world of mine emerged from elements of my own concrete existence that were once perfectly inscrutable. In fact, many of the experiences were least adapted to any abstract operations that would permit me to translate them into clear, direct thought. The fundamental trait of my theater works is that I do make this attempt, however, and this perhaps explains why my plays are so difficult to produce. But by the same token they therefore portray real existence more powerfully than any of my philosophical writing ever could. I am sure when it comes to analysis, a critic or commentator will find himself genuinely more challenged by my plays.

In my plays I need not attempt any authentic comprehension; I simply have to confine myself to reporting a course of events more or less faithfully. I was able to observe this personally for the first time last summer in London. A group had performed my *Chemin de Crête* (Ariadne), and afterwards some impudent critics complained about what they thought was a poor presentation. They felt it was too difficult to determine whether the heroine was sympathetic or not. But I have always felt that that was exactly my point; the ambiguity is the essence of the entire play, and actress Ellen Cherry deserves high commendation for her ability to understand and portray the point dramatically. If she had acted in any other way she would have misinterpreted my intentions.

Keeping this in mind I would like to speak briefly about the play most often produced not only in France, but also abroad, especially in Germany. I am not about to say it represents one of my finest efforts, but it does yield some valuable information about what I am trying to do on the stage.

Although I am sure most of you are familiar with the plot, for those of you who are not I would like to cite Louis Chaigne's short summary of it:

> The Evangelical pastor Claude Lemoine is an eminent citizen of Paris; he has made a brilliant career for himself, and he enjoys everyone's respect. And life would certainly have run its sweet course, if a tragedy did not turn up a skeleton in the family closet. As it turns out, in the first years of their marriage his wife, Ednée, had an affair with one of their neighbors by the name of Michel Sandler. She conceived and later gave birth to a daughter, Osmonde. Since Ednée had no idea of what would become of her otherwise, she did not forfeit her marriage. Instead she admitted everything to her husband, and he in turn readily forgave her.
>
> Now, twenty years later, Michel suddenly returns, worn out from licentious living and marked for death. But before he dies he wants to meet his daughter; she, in the meantime, is under the strict supervision of her mother. Ednée strictly reprimands her for visiting too often the father of two young girls now living apart from their mother because she is confined to an insane asylum. Under the pretext of looking after the children, Osmonde is a frequent house guest.

On the surface the play hardly seems to distinguish itself from any one of the countless other plays that have been produced over the past three-quarters of a century. But this is certainly no way to approach the matter. It could perhaps be said, for example, that I am making use of Ibsen's form; that here, just as in *Rosmersholm* (one of my favorite plays), the action deals with a past situation that suddenly encroaches upon the present. While I have no intention of denying Ibsen's influence on my own craft, I would simply like to point out that in *Un Homme de Dieu* and *Chemin de Crête* I have incorporated elements that are not likely to be found in Ibsen. My reference is to the general questioning that takes place, gradually disclosing the abyss of uncertainty that exists for the characters in the drama, as well as for the audience. Take *Un Homme de Dieu* as an illustration. In two successive scenes Ednée finds time to question everything; through an unguarded remark of her mother-in-law she learns that Claude was going through a period of religious doubt before he became aware of her unfaithfulness. After he forgave her, he did not rediscover his faith—since he had never actually lost it—but he did regain confidence in his vocation. It looked as though his forgiving her was nothing more than a professional success. I purposely say "professional," for who had actually forgiven her? The man? The husband? Or perhaps the pastor? If it was the pastor, we are compelled to ask whether this caused the man in him to disappear, that is, the man and his love. Had this lover ever really existed? Out of this mist of uncertainty comes the tragic cry of Ednée at the conclusion of the first act: "If you did not forgive out of love, what do you want me to make of your forgiveness?"

Her deep suspicion becomes even darker in the sequel. Loathing the prospect of ever seeing Michel Sandler again, she is horrified when Claude suggests: "It is our duty to receive him; it is a trial we dare not shrink from." The attitude and language of the professional cleric? This might seem to prove Claude is genuinely incapable of the normal and natural reactions of a man in love with his wife who learns of the proximate presence of her one-time paramour. Love in this context, however, is dangerously ambiguous. Is there no unjealous love? Even if there were, Ednée would be terribly suspicious of it, since she cannot help seeing the professional preacher behind all of Claude's protestations.

Claude is nonplused by Ednée's refusal. Nevertheless, the meeting does take place, but it only increases Ednée's uneasiness and undermines drastically her self-confidence.

Marked as he is for death, Michel Sandler admits that he loved

Ednée more dearly than she suspected; in fact, as it turns out, he had even proposed that they elope. At the time, however, Ednée gave Michel to understand that she mistrusted him, while interiorly what she really feared were the consequences of such an act. When she consequently resolved to tell her husband everything, she was sure he would take the whole affair quite nobly, and yet this very nobility, she also knew, would be the greatest hindrance to her genuinely renouncing her affair with Sandler.

In scrupulously examining her past, she now discovers that she was unafraid when she made her confession to Claude, and this precipitates the question whether Claude had ever been a husband to her at all. Her complaints against him grow more insistent, until, finally, she dares accuse him of things that touch his very being, not only his conduct. Like a mortally wounded animal he cries out: "Be quiet; you are destroying me!"

Today, perhaps more clearly than when I wrote the play, I recognize how incapable the characters are of coping with their own past. That is a fact of life itself. The scene I still find the most deeply moving is in the fourth act where these unhappy people discover that they actually have no idea of what happened in the past or how they felt. Claude asks: "Were we really in love with one another? We don't remember; you simply trusted a glance and committed your life. And what did this glance promise? In any event the mysterious promise was not kept; that's the story of our life together."

Here I am now in 1959, at the end of an intellectual journey I could hardly have foreseen when I wrote *Un Homme de Dieu*, and I genuinely believe I could show my characters a few things, provided we could meet face to face and they would confide in me. I would tell Claude: You should realize the pardon you granted Ednée is only real in the light of the present, as an actuality. It certainly is not an object you can manipulate and subject to chemical analysis, as if to ask: What *was* my act really? You were unjust because you did not silence Ednée at once; you let her become infected with suspicion. You were too scrupulous, as you yourself found out, but too late.

Insofar as I can allow myself an opinion about my characters,

I would perhaps judge Ednée more harshly than any of the others. In the words of her brother-in-law, a physician: "She appears to be sleeping her life away." The play is the story of her awakening, but with the attendant awakening of devastating powers heretofore locked up within her—they are now turned loose, first against her husband, then against herself.

I admit the play is gloomy. To that extent it is more like Strindberg than like Ibsen. Yet I have to confess I knew practically nothing about Strindberg when I wrote it.

A comparison of this piece with *Le Quatuor en Fa dièze* reveals a certain affinity between Clair and Ednée.

While I eventually did come to be connected with Protestantism, in consequence of my marriage, nothing would be more false than to see *Un Homme de Dieu* as a satire on Protestantism. I was always pleased with the Protestant milieu I came to know through my various enjoyable relationships, and at the time my play was taking shape I had not the slightest notion of one day converting to Catholicism; in fact, I was not even in the least familiar with it.

By mistaking or ignoring the publication date, still others have interpreted the play as an apology for the celibacy of Catholic priests. At that time, no thought was further from my mind. But if someone is really bent on discovering a practical application let me suggest this: The marriage of a pastor is something quite different from an ordinary marriage; the wife of a pastor has special obligations; she must be bound with heart and soul to the religious life of her husband. Otherwise, these marriages end in disaster. This particular conclusion is based on concrete evidence I had in my possession when I wrote the piece.

Why did I write it? This question provides a welcome opportunity to say that nothing is more important for a dramatic work than the absence of definite purpose. A dramatic work must never be written to support an idea the author wants to hammer into the heads of his audience. The dignity of a dramatic work can only be preserved if the author's rejection of any outside determination of its actual objective is absolute and unconditional.

But one may ask whether the devout philosopher Gabriel Marcel, particularly the Catholic convert of 1929, has any right to this opinion. He may have been able to think like this when he wrote *Un Homme de Dieu* and *La Chapelle Ardente,* but can he still maintain such a position today?

It is a valid question, and I hasten to say "yes," I still share my earlier conviction; in fact, it is the key to my latest works, as well as the bellicose conviction and coordinating element of my weekly drama review. Take my second-last published play, *Croissez et Multipliez,* which netted me violent attacks from many quarters and even difficulties with the Holy Office.

As in all my other plays, I begin with a sketch, a sympathetic sketch of a human being, this time a woman. The odd thing is that I have never actually met such a woman, and yet after I "invented" her, she impressed me as being irresistible. As has happened so many times before, my mental anticipation was soon confirmed by experience. Her name was Agnes; she had married Thierry Courteuil soon after the end of World War II. Thierry had been a prisoner of war for five years; he was a devout Catholic and wanted to establish a good Christian family with many children. As for Agnes, she had grown up in the overprotected and freethinking atmosphere of a diplomat's home and was attracted by the profound simplicity and devotion she found in Thierry. When she married him, I am sure she could not have anticipated what lay before her: five complicated pregnancies and the difficulties she was to have with her husband on account of a certain Abbé Petitpaul. The Abbé was a close friend of Thierry's since their days together in a prisoner of war camp, and now he is Thierry's pastor and the religious advisor to his family.

As the play opens, Agnes is expecting her sixth child. She is affronted by the indifference of her husband and of the Abbé; in fact, she has turned against life itself. She sees it as a mere capacity for absurd proliferation, and nothing else. At this point she is shocked to meet her brother, Bruno, who during the many intervening years has been living the life of a celibate. Of all people, she thought Bruno would be the most able to understand her loathing for the flesh that has condemned her to a situation of permanent pregnancy. But he does not; on the contrary, he holds her in contempt and treats her like a heretic. One might be inclined to think that Bruno is only a well-versed theologian, but the truth of the matter is something deeper and more embarrassing. You see, Bruno, too, has suffered the sting of the flesh. He admits that at the wedding of his best friend he was pestered by erotic feelings toward him. It was then that he had decided to become a religious.

Perhaps here an explanatory note is in order. I have often been accused of claiming that every religious vocation has a homosexual foundation. Needless to say, the assertion is absurd. In the case of *Un Homme de Dieu*, such a generalization would lead to an equally false conclusion. A dramatist is not allowed to peddle any general ideas. Everything takes place in the encounter between individual persons. I know from experience, better than many another, that there are mothers of ten or twelve children who would not be able to make the least bit of sense out of Agnes' conflict. I know, too, that religious vocations do not generally spring from the recognition of some abnormal tendency. But is that any reason why I cannot present persons like Agnes and Bruno on the stage, even though, admittedly, in some way they are exceptional? As extreme cases I am inclined to feel they can arouse and stimulate our own thinking. A very well-known Catholic psychiatrist thanked me for writing this play. He said that not a day passed that he could not confirm the validity of my analysis. This testimony I regard as the highest approval of my work.

If I were asked why I wrote such a disturbing play, I would have to say: As I understand the theater, it has to be disquieting. And this brings me to an essential consideration: My dramas are beyond doubt the most disturbing of my writings. Yet, if my work were strictly limited to writing of this sort, I would be deeply suspicious of it myself. Maybe I never made that point clear before, but it does, in any case, afford an insight into who I am. From now on, anyone who studies my work, and above all my philosophical thought, without prejudice, should never neglect to see the key; otherwise, he will be jeopardizing a true understanding of my intentions.

Now, I said even I would be suspicious of my work if I only considered the philosophical side of it. It would look as if I had been building during my whole life a comfortable refuge in lieu of having the necessary courage to come to grips with the tragic and disturbing aspects of concrete existence. I might even add, certain "well-meaning" Catholics might be inclined to draw me into their camp, if they overlooked my theatrical productions. A young Italian I know made this mistake. In his doctoral dissertation on my philosophy written for the University of Bologna, he propounded a simplified version of my thought which I simply cannot accept. If, for example, you read carefully the chapter "Phenomenology of Hope" in *Homo Viator,* you will readily see that I hardly underestimate the possibilities of despair that life and the world conceal. And it goes without saying that I can better accentuate the possibility of despair, of betrayal and of denial in my plays.

Is despair, then, the final message of my dramas? Certainly not. And yet I have written some plays—in my estimation some very valuable plays—where I offer no hopeful solution. The story of *La Chapelle Ardente* is a case in point. Having lost her son at the front, Aline Fortier lives a life of perpetual mourning. Her sorrow even separates her from her husband, whom she somehow holds partially responsible for Raymond's death. Raymond's widow, Mireille, lives with the Fortier family. Aline requires more than Mireille's mere presence; she needs her conjugal fidelity to Raymond, as if Raymond ceased to be dead on account of it. She carefully keeps from Mireille everything that could possibly give her life a new direction. For example, there is a handsome young man in the neighborhood, Robert Chanteuil, who seems to be interested in Mireille, but Aline sees him as nothing but an enemy, threatening to capture Mireille's love and encourage her unfaithfulness to Raymond. But at the same time Aline entertains little hope of keeping Mireille from marrying, so she chooses the "lesser evil" and recommends a nephew, André Verdet. He loves Mireille and is exempted from military service for reasons of health. But he does not venture to propose, and if Mireille is to marry him, it will have to be out of pity, not love. In that case, no shadow would fall on the demanding lover which Raymond has come to be. It was not the real Raymond whom the grim reaper had taken, but Aline's

Raymond, the idolized son, whom her memory had managed to reincarnate. Aline uses the most precious traits as well as the weaknesses of Mireille to serve the ends of her one consuming passion. And in the end the young girl does marry the sickly young man she does not love.

Has Aline acted perfidiously? When this charge is made, she rejects it indignantly, and with perfect candor. But is she really honest? No! She simply cannot bear to see Mireille love any other man but Raymond. Still, she is unable to recognize this will of hers for what it is; she conceals it behind her attitude of insincere self-assurance. In her mind Mireille could not possibly be in love with Chanteuil. The girl simply yields to her own self-deception.

Having thus succeeded in bringing the marriage about, Aline, through an impropriety, then goes and destroys the delicate balance the couple in the meantime has managed to establish. In the presence of her husband, she tells Mireille of Chanteuil's death in an automobile accident. Her cautious phrasing designed to minimize the shock only serves to arouse in Mireille's husband the thought that she is deeply affected by the news; he suspects she married him only out of pity, perhaps even because she expected that their union would be short-lived. Aline feels her trickery has been unmasked, so in desperation she leaves the house. Suspecting she might resort to something drastic, Mireille and André have no alternative but to bring her back. They will never be free of her again as long as they live.

I personally think Aline should be pitied rather than hated. She is the embodiment of that pain resulting from the loss of all hope. This is precisely the reason I think the play acts as an admonition. It brings to the surface another kind of pain—one which only hope can change into something beyond itself and make it fruitful. At the same time it becomes apparent that not everyone can be saved by the power of believing and hopeful souls. Some remain blind and enslaved, and we have to listen to their heartrending complaints. It seems the reason they exist is to remind us that the ultimate truth is indeed light, but everyone is not given to behold this light on earth.

It is likewise impossible to prove that despairing souls are seeing things falsely. Our own limitations require that we bear the burden of our own human potentiality and work to master it for ourselves and for those dear to us, without deluding ourselves as to the influence our eventual victory will have on others.

Similar observations could be made concerning *Chemin de Crête,* even though it is a much richer play than *La Chapelle Ardente.* By that I mean to say that these two somber plays, still my favorites, have not lost any of their meaning in light of the subsequent publication of *Le Monde Cassé* or *Coeurs Avides,* where the horizon brightens sufficiently to suggest a tangible solution. This latter fact is based on a somewhat more difficult train of thought—I shall now try to clarify it.

Every existential philosopher is bound to acknowledge at least some insoluble paradoxes. I use the word "paradox" designedly; it is a crucial notion in the thinking of Kierkegaard.

It is difficult not to yield to the temptation to advance a proposition like this: One who believes, even without seeing, senses what will be given to him when he is finally liberated from his earthly bondage. It is similarly difficult not to maintain that, while the believer cannot actually surpass the non-believer, he can at least surpass the person who remains a victim of doubt and anxiety.

Such self-assurance is questionable, I admit. Aline's pain reflects an existential self-assurance that is beyond the ken of any believer who has not suffered the anxiety and experienced the uprooting that the death of her son meant for Aline. We know as a fact that many of the faithful, yes, even priests, are incapable of helping someone who has been plunged into such an abyss of misery. The faithful and priests, in this case, have not "surpassed" the sufferer in any real way, discounting of course the naive attempt to compare intelligences. The only one who can be of assistance at such moments is someone who has been dragged equally deep into the abyss we call pain. Only then can he reach the one who is suffering and share his experience. And yet, this sympathy alone is not enough; it still has to be sublimated and made alive, so to speak.

This intensification is not knowledge; it is evidence embodied in love. In my opinion, such love is grace; but it is very difficult to represent it in drama. Nor have I ever tried to do so directly. As in my philosophical writings, I have to try to approach the problem through paraphrase; but certainly my approach must be extremely concrete, as in the conclusion of *Rome n'est plus dans Rome, L'Emissaire, Signe de la Croix,* or in the last scene of *Croissez et Multipliez.*

I am purposely going to return to my controversial *Croissez et Multipliez,* for I think it contains most of the significant statements of my work. I will take up the thread where we left off. As I have already said, Abbé Petitpaul has unconsciously but most imprudently meddled in the strictly personal sphere of marital intimacy. He is a man of goodwill, and as soon as he becomes aware of his error, he resolves to withdraw from the scene. He acted wrongly in not helping Thierry stand on his own two feet, to grow into a real father of a family instead of remaining a child, a good child, but stupid. With perfect naiveté Thierry tells his wife that the woman, a relative, who had taken care of the children in her absence had thrown her arms around his neck and he had suffered a sensual temptation. What had deterred him from yielding was the thought of the grief he would have caused the Abbé. That leads to a final discussion between Agnes, Thierry, and the Abbé. Allow me to recount the gist of it.

Abbé: My friends, I think I am beginning to see things more clearly now. What the Church here, as everywhere, really demands is heroism. But in daily life we are hardly prepared to play the hero. Heroism is an indefinite potentiality reserved for such momentous situations as war, persecution, and the like. Consequently, from day to day falsehood and hypocrisy take root in us.

Thierry: I don't think I understand . . .

Abbé: Sure you do. Remember our gatherings in the Rue Saint-Placide? I admit it isn't pleasant for me to recall them now . . . but this sharing of goods, this mutual sympathy, as the people in the Moral Rearmament call it . . . surely that implies a brotherliness that could be something beautiful. But then there are also these little technical concessions, the miserable exchange of petty experiences . . . and, furthermore, there is the rhythm method recommended by churchmen, in effect telling people to choose the few days of the month when the risk is minimal. . . . these loopholes have been tolerated and it is probably wrong. Radicalism means nothing if it isn't heroic. But heroism excludes petty tricks. Anyway, does anyone have the right to require heroism? I don't think anyone would dare say so nowadays. We are always quick to accommodate ourselves to the world. In fact, the more often one goes to communion, the more necessary it becomes. Gone are the days when confession was an annual housecleaning. Even you, Thierry, though you are quite innocent in this regard, have not acted honorably; you have never wanted to see the dramatic reality of the world. And what about us priests? Are we any more honest? Who knows, perhaps our stern attitude simply hides some unadmitted resentment.

Thierry: Yes, and the Church?

Abbé: Of course the Church stands above this wretchedness; but what is the Church here on earth? Yes, I know what the handbooks say. And we are supposed to be satisfied with them. But there come moments when one just can't anymore.

Thierry: You frighten me.

Abbé (sadly): Don't worry. Things will return to normal. The lid is already back in place, and the next time we meet I'll be speaking in a different tone. Except for extraordinary cases, do you really think a family can be heroic?

(Silence)

Agnes: I know my answer. I went from enthusiasm to goodwill, then to resignation and, finally, to rebellion. Heroism cannot exist without a faith that is so strong it is scarcely imaginable. For a while we live a conscientious married life, and then. . . . If I decide to stay maybe I could resign myself again, this time on deeper level . . .

Abbé: Agnes is being honest. What about you, Thierry?

Thierry: I know I'm not a hero, but I always hoped I wouldn't become narrow-minded. I hate the very mention of the word.

Abbé: I know that you thought daily communion would guarantee you against conformism, but you have been trying to burn both ends of the candle at once: you did not have to deny yourself anything just because you are cut out for monogamy . . .

Agnes (bitterly): Don't you think it would have been better if he had given in to his temptations? At least he would have lost his wonderful peace of conscience!

Thierry: Let me say it again; what I do could perhaps salvage our marriage; for it is quite obvious neither you nor I am about to rise to heroism. Let's get back to real life, where there is no *fata morgana,* where one sins, repents, and then . . . sins, repents, and starts all over again.

Abbé (very earnestly): Those are terrible thoughts, and I forbid you to pursue them any further. If the virtue we think we are practicing is indecisive and ambiguous—if virtue is no longer virtue—then sin is death.

Thierry (pained): Agnes, if you could so much as think of a lapse on my part and consider it blameless, for that matter desirable, then I stand condemned. If I were to yield to you, even my faith wouldn't be enough to prevent my regarding it as suicide.

Agnes: No, I don't think that is true; for who knows, maybe we are obeying principles that were discovered thousands of years ago in which we no longer believe.

Thierry (sadly): The flesh is not a rag that one may soil as he pleases. It will rise on the last day.

Agnes: You mean there is no solution?

Abbé (seriously): No! Everyone has to pray that he will find his own way, and I believe—it makes me tremble to say this —that even the pope and his associates have to pray. I don't think they are permitted to confine themselves to empty formulas either. No one is exempt from understanding, considering and praying.

(Before departing, the Abbé pronounces the following prayer.)

Abbé (simply but devoutly): O Lord, grant us the strength to examine our conscience without disgust, to recognize the significance of our mistakes, for they all result from egotism, sloth and blindness and are their inescapable consequence. Before you, Lord God, I confess that I should have enlightened my friends, that I was a poor advisor, that I have led them into temptation. Lord, they are now firmly determined to resume life together, to obey your law without knowing their strength. Help them, provide them with a priest whose counsels will not amount to meddling. I have erred.

I introduced this scene to indicate the limitations a dramatist has to impose upon himself. If he offers a solution, he oversteps the bounds of his assignment. Here, as in *Emissaire* and other plays, I want to clarify an almost hopeless situation in the light of a truth that is inseparable from love. I am not afraid to admit that this conclusion is non-conformist; consequently, I expect it will and must annoy anyone who believes that rigid formulas are sufficient to solve any problem. But while my solution might be non-conformist, it does not call into question my basic conviction that marriage produces a certain kind of holiness. How can it be preserved? One has to pray. But prayer and its fruit lie beyond where a dramatist may go without committing sacrilege. If he is a Christian, all he can and must do is guide the soul in such a way that it will devote itself more freely to him whose judgment no human being can predict.

These remarks ought to indicate the precise place of my theatrical works with regard to my other writings. Their secret motivation is my impatience with the kind of schematizing that philosophers—and professors of philosophy in particular—find difficult to resist. That is why at the beginning of nearly all my plays there stands a "Yes, but. . . ." It does not reflect a morbid delight in complexity and vagueness, because the obscurity can never exist except in the background; it dares not in any way prejudice the clarity of speech or our choice of a dramatic medium. It is a question here of indirect love. It may seem surprising, but let me quote a saying of Terence that impressed me deeply in my school days: *Nihil humani a me alienum puto* (Nothing human, I believe, is foreign to me).

I am not about to stone anyone or condemn any situation. All of them deserve to be understood and to gain our sympathy. There are cases when the honorable course of action means acknowledging that a judgment is impossible, in which case we can only hope and pray we will be able to find an answer—coming from a greater distance and a greater height than our world could ever reach. Consequently, no one can, like a childish spectator, expect a dramatist to give us only those palliatives that calm and satisfy us. He has to be able to maintain his personal honesty. But thank God it is possible to push forward to a point where light appears—a light that will be recognized by the persons involved in the action as well as by the audience. It is always a great joy for me to sense that even in the case of the most daring insights that the actors are called upon to voice there suddenly arises a mysterious clarity in their minds and, through them, in the mind of the audience. That happens, for example, in *Dard,* in *L'Emissaire,* and in *Signe de la Croix.*

Not only as dramatist, but also as a theater critic who has read and seen plays of every description, I venture to say that the duty, domain and office of a dramatist are not easy to define. Therefore, I offer a comparison. What Rilke said about the task of a writer is well known, not only in the *Duisenen Elegien* but also in one of his most important letters to Hulevicz. "The lively, living things ordered to our knowledge are in ruins and can never be restored. We are perhaps the last to have known them. We have the responsibility for not only keeping fresh the remembrance of them (that would be too little and too uncertain), but also of preserving their human worth." I might almost add—and this thought strikes me for the first time—that this task rests principally on the shoulders of dramatists, for they write not about things but about people. For nowadays even people are not less threatened than the simple and familiar things—the house of one's birth, the grape-arbor and the spring. In those moments when it seemed that I was deliberately writing myself into a scene, I detected a secret feeling of mission. It suffices, and must suffice, that through this mission of mine a few of my fellow human beings feel they are understood and know that it is their deeds and their sufferings I have expressed. If I can do this, my play has been successful.

Again, I want to emphasize the relationship between drama and music; they are intimately related to one another, even though, I admit, the dramatist's media of expression are incomparably less pure and much more subject to flaws than those of the musician. Still, I say without hesitation that those scenes in my plays which I like best and which constitute the acme of my dramatic work are the ones where I feel the audience is being swept along as if carried away by a stirring movement of some musical composition. That was true, for example, in the closing scenes of *Coeurs Avides* and *Signe de la Croix*.

This lecture is nothing more than a brief outline. My most important objective was to warn you against any and all one-sided interpretations of my work. The commonly asserted contrast between my work and that of Sartre has done much to cloud the issue. In any case, the most important element of my work is neglected unless the existence of the "restless heart" mentioned by St. Augustine in his *Confessions* is clearly recognized as my motivating force from beginning to end. I could have complicated this discussion a great deal, if I had included my comedies, particularly *La Dimension Florestan*, where the main character, the philosopher Dolch, or rather his language, exhibits some features of Martin Heidegger—but let me say immediately, it was not meant to be a caricature of the famous philosopher by any means.

How does my comedy fit into the broad perspectives I have indicated? It, too, fits into the schema of "Yes, but . . ."; it, too, is "disturbing." *Divertissement Posthume* is a burlesque play and yet extremely disquieting. Basically, the play is a warning against the deceptive tendency to imagine life as one musical harmony. I wanted to remind people with fierce insistence of the disharmony that prevails in and around us. For this reason *Divertissement Posthume* is as non-conformist as it could possibly be. On the periphery of *Dimension Florestan* there is evidence that satire can also end, if not in orthodoxy, at least in an orderliness that accords with human limitations.

Anyone who reads my dramas without prejudice ought to conclude that they preserve the primacy of truth and that at the same time they show that a mysterious, hidden bond exists between love and truth, expressed more often by allusion than by clear statement.

Finally, there is one element which up to now only very few have been able to discover, namely, the absolute primacy of simple and chaste hearts. The word "simple" is to be understood, not in the social, but in the ethical and religious sense. I have in mind particularly Aunt Lena in *Signe de la Croix*. She is an elderly, faithful Jewess who fled Vienna after the Anschluss of

1938 and nevertheless lost her life in a Nazi gas chamber. Naturally, the complicated and sometimes distorted characters can and must reach a plane that is only accessible to pure and simple hearts, and sometimes by different and more or less tortuous routes. And so, I feel I am closer to Chekhov and Dostoievski than to Strindberg.

In conclusion, I ask those of you who are interested in my work and for the most part know only my philosophical writings to study my dramas, too. For in them, whatever the intrinsic value of my plays may be, lies the unique contribution in which I best recognize myself as I approach the end of my life.